THE FILMS OF GENE KELLY

SONG AND DANCE MAN

THE FILMS OF GENE KELLY

SONG AND DANCE MAN

by TONY THOMAS

Foreword by FRED ASTAIRE

THE CITADEL PRESS   Secaucus, N. J.

Second paperbound printing, 1979

Copyright © 1974 by Tony Thomas
All rights reserved
Published by Citadel Press
A division of Lyle Stuart, Inc.
120 Enterprise Ave., Secaucus, N.J. 07094
In Canada: George J. McLeod Limited
73 Bathurst St., Toronto 2B, Ont.
Manufactured in the United States of America by
Halliday Lithograph Corp., West Hanover, Mass.
Designed by A. Christopher Simon
Library of Congress catalog card number: 73-90949

ISBN 0-8065-0543-5

To the memory of Jeanne Coyne Kelly

ACKNOWLEDGMENTS

For the help I received in putting this book together I am grateful for the kindness of the following people: to Fred Astaire, Vincente Minnelli, John Green and Rudy Behlmer; to Mildred Simpson and her staff at the library of the Academy of Motion Picture Arts and Sciences in Los Angeles; to Gerald Pratley and his staff at the Ontario Film Institute in Toronto; and to Glen Hunter and the staff of the Theatre Section of the Metropolitan Toronto Central Library. My thanks also to Lois McClelland, secretary to Mr. Kelly, and to Dale Olson of Rogers, Cowan and Brenner, Inc. (Beverly Hills). For aid in collecting the photographs I gratefully thank John Lebold, Paula Klaw of *Movie Star News* (New York), Larry Edmund's Bookshop (Hollywood), Cherokee Bookshop (Hollywood), Diane Goodrich and Eddie Brandt. Many of the photographs are from Mr. Kelly's private collection and for his permission to use them I am most particularly grateful.

Tony Thomas

CONTENTS

THE FILMS OF GENE KELLY

SONG AND DANCE MAN

FOREWORD

BY FRED ASTAIRE

Writing a foreword about Gene Kelly is not all that easy for me. I mean there would naturally be some opinions—"Oh, of course, he had to say that." Many people think of dancers as being too aware or jealous of one another. Such is not the case here. I think I know Gene pretty well. He has his easier, lighter moods and also his very serious moments, which are only natural with an artistic temperament.

I worked with him in one movie—a massive MGM production, *Ziegfeld Follies,* filmed in 1944–45. We got along fine with the many discussions, not particularly arguments, that are bound to occur when you're in rehearsal together on a creative basis. It's "How about this?" or "No—not that" sort of thing that goes on, but I don't recall that we ran into any particular obstacles. I had heard that he was sometimes tough to work with, being a perfectionist and all that. And when you

1

Astaire and Kelly doing "The Babbitt and the Bromide" in *Ziegfeld Follies*

A recent photo of Fred Astaire and Gene Kelly

have two so-called perfectionists belting away at each other, you might get some kind of fireworks when it applies to a couple of hoofers. That gave me some concern.

However, Gene was not tough with me. He was very respectful—maybe because of my seniority in years. Besides, I was doing my utmost not to be objectionable because I was aware of the fact that he was a very strong and gymnastic young man. I had seen him pick up Ed Sullivan once and carry him off stage like a suitcase. Well—joking aside, as I said there were really no obstacles that deterred us from arriving at what I think proved to be an enjoyable and successful song-and-dance version of a number called "The Babbitt and the Bromide," which was originally written by the Gershwins, George and Ira, for my sister Adele and me in our Broadway stage production musical comedy *Funny Face* in 1927.

Doing that number with Gene in a totally different form was, of course, a challenge for both of us but we always felt that it did work out well, largely due to his creative contributions, and I feel that it became somewhat of a memorable screen musical item.

That was the only thing we did together.

Kelly is a man of multiple talents—dancer—singer—actor—director—producer—completely engulfed when at his work. His many successes speak for themselves.

Gene is also a devoted family man. My respect for him as a person and an artist is unbounded.

While Kelly and Donald O'Connor were making *Singin' in the Rain* they were visited by Fred Astaire, who was working on *The Belle of New York* on the next sound stage.

Photo by Gjon Mili

This strobe photo was taken
by Gjon Mili at the time
Kelly was doing *Cover Girl*.

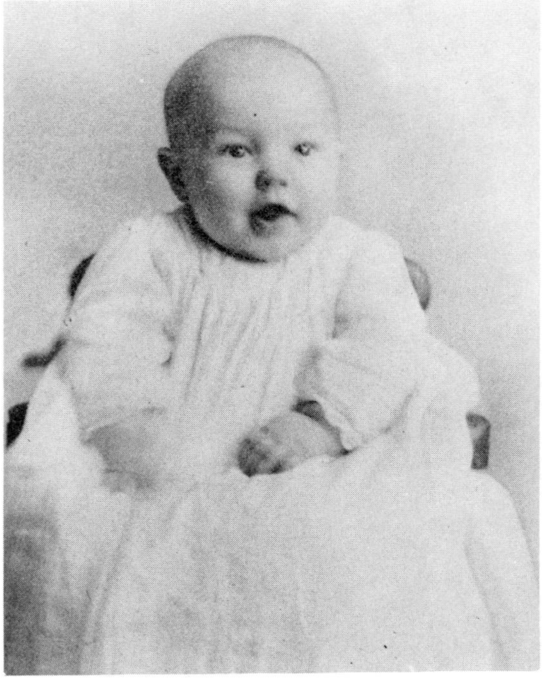

Gene Kelly—his first role

THE LONELINESS OF THE LONG-DISTANCE DANCER

A conspicuous peculiarity in the history of Hollywood is the emergence of only two male dancers as major stars. Through all the decades of high productivity and the popularity of thousands of players of every kind only Fred Astaire and Gene Kelly among the song-and-dance men have scaled the heights of film fame and stayed there. This inevitable tandem reference has lead to perpetual comparison, and an assumption that they have more in common than is actually the case. Both as men and as dancers Astaire and Kelly are more different than they are alike. In their only performance together, a routine in the MGM revue, *Ziegfeld Follies,* they were directed by Vincente Minnelli, who also directed Kelly in *An American in Paris* and Astaire in *The Band Wagon.* In Minnelli's eyes: "Gene bases a lot of his work on ballet, combing modern and tap dancing with ballet movements in great strength and athleticism. Fred, of course, is light as air and has a style completely his own—it hasn't been approached by any other dancer. He's a shy, retiring man who doesn't like to talk about his work whereas Gene is more earthy, very gregarious and eloquent on the subject of dancing. What they have in common is perfectionism, the capacity to work long and hard to get the smallest detail right. They are both originators, both have devised marvelous dance material for movies and each is, in his own way, a great showman."

By the time Gene Kelly arrived in Hollywood at the end of 1941 Fred Astaire had been in films for nine years and occupied an unrivaled position of affection and esteem. Once Kelly had established himself he began hearing references to himself as "another Astaire," not that he was obviously similar to the older dancer, but because the public could find no other simple way to describe him.

8

Age four

James Patrick and Harriet Kelly, with their children
Fred, James, Louise, Gene and Harriet Joan

Louise, Gene, Harriet Joan, James and Fred

9

There was never any rivalry because there was never any competition between them. It never bothered Kelly that he was, particularly in his early years in films, continually compared with Astaire: "I was delighted to be compared with Fred because he's a genius in his own right and a man can do worse than being compared with the best. Anyone dancing on the screen today who doesn't admit his debt to Astaire is either a fool or a liar. I used to envy his cool, aristocratic style, so intimate and contained but I was wise enough to know it wasn't for me. Fred wears top hat, white tie and tails to the manner born—I put them on and look like a truckdriver. We've been good friends all these years but even if we weren't I think we would have gotten together now and then just to commiserate with one other. We were like two men on a desert island, the only ones aware of our mutual problem—trying to make dances come alive before the cameras as a bored crew stood and watched. Stage dancers couldn't understand what concerned us. Ours was a kind of splendid isolation."

According to Kelly the shortage of dancer-actors is due to the long and totally absorbing training necessary in order to dance professionally. "A dancer works so hard at training his anatomy that he doesn't give much time to training the rest of himself. Nobody asks, 'Why aren't there any violinists who have become movie stars?' and yet a dancer can spend as much time perfecting his craft as a violinist. And after years of training he discovers he has trouble saying 'hello' on the stage. It's a rare dancer who can hold his own in an acting role. This concentration on perfecting dancing to the exclusion of other areas of being an entertainer is strange to anyone who isn't involved. The point is simply that nature is against you—by the time you've learned your craft your anatomy is starting to run down. The older you get as a dancer the harder it is to grind up the physical forces. A writer can still pound a typewriter at fifty—an actor is usually better at fifty than he was at thirty, but it's the reverse with a dancer. Just when he is experienced and mature he starts running out of steam. The dancer's life is probably the shortest artistic life in the world and you have to face that fact when you get into it."

The ideal performer is the man who combines the discipline of the dancer with the emotional expertise of the actor, but such men are rare—and made all the more rare by an unpredictable public. "There are better dancers than Astaire or myself, and certainly better actors and singers but the public won't have them. The trouble with movies is that no matter how talented a person is, he will flop unless the public takes to his personality. As a director my eyes are peeled all the time for some young man who can act, sing and dance, and who is personable enough to build a show around but even if you found such a person there is no guarantee that the public would accept him."

When Gene Kelly first appeared in Hollywood pictures it was often remarked that he seemed a little like James Cagney. In Kelly's estimation the reason for this comparison is George M. Cohan: "Cohan set the style for the American song-and-dance man—a tough, cheeky, Irish style. Cohan wasn't a great dancer, but he had wonderful timing and a winning personality. He influenced a whole breed of American actors, including Cagney, Spencer Tracy and Pat O'Brien—and when Cagney did Cohan in *Yankee Doodle Dandy* he was an improvement on the original. Cohan *was* the American theatre up until the impact of Eugene O'Neill, and I have a lot of Cohan in me. It's an Irish quality, a jaw-jutting, up-on-the-toes cockiness—which is a good quality for a male dancer to have. And it's a legacy from George M. Cohan."

Eugene Curran Kelly was born in the Highland Park district of Pittsburgh, Pennsylvania, on August 23rd, 1912. He was the third of five children —Harriet, James, Eugene, Louise and Fred—born to James Patrick Kelly and his wife Harriet, née Curran. Kelly senior, born in Peterborough, Ontario, of Irish parents, was employed by the Columbia Gramophone Company as a salesman and held a good position until the economic crash of 1929, when he was dismissed. Recalls Kelly: "Until then it had been a good, comfortable, lower-middle-class home and I look back on it as a very happy childhood. With the Depression we had to pull in our belts but we kids were in our teens by then and we pitched in and got through that period better than many. It was a marvelous family. My father was an easygoing man with the usual Canadian love of ice hockey, and on freezing days he would flood the back yard and have his three boys out there shooting the puck around. By the time I was in high school I had my letter as a peewee halfback and at fifteen I was working out with a semipro ice hockey team, the Pittsburgh Yellow Jackets. I was encouraged to take it up professionally, but I wasn't that interested. However, much of my style as a dancer springs from that early training in ice hockey."

Kelly's emergence as a dancer is due his mother, a lively lady with a strong interest in the theatrical arts and a firm believer in the "American Dream" precept of cultural and social improvement. "She loved dancing and she sent my older brother James and I—I was about eight then—to the Fairgreaves School in the East End of Pittsburgh to take dancing lessons. We didn't like it much and we were continually involved in fistfights with the neighborhood boys who called us sissies. Strong-willed as my mother was, she had to give in, and I didn't dance again until I was fifteen. By that time I'd been on several athletic teams and I wasn't afraid of anyone calling me names. Also, it had come to my attention that girls liked dancing and any guy who could dance had a head start. So I went back to Miss Fairgreaves and asked her if she could teach me some steps. I found I had great adaptability for it, so I got a tap routine together and did it in the high school show. This made me quite a hero with the girls, and I had no trouble with boys because I was a sports nut—hockey, football, baseball, gymnastics, everything."

Gene Kelly spent his first year of high school at the Sacred Heart School, then three years at Peabody High in his final year appearing in several school plays. In 1929 he enrolled at Pennsylvania State College to study journalism but the economic crash also made it necessary for him to get a job to supplement the family finances. He first worked for the YMCA as an instructor in gymnastics. At the same time, he and his brother Fred, three years younger, worked up dance routines in order to appear in amateur talent contests and pick up occasional prize money. The following year Kelly began a course in economics at the University of Pittsburgh, later switching his interest to law. He graduated with a Bachelor of Arts degree in 1933.

At Penn State he had joined the college theatrical club and discovered an increasing taste for entertaining and at the University he devised a dance act with a friend named Jim Barry. In the summer of 1931 Kelly was hired as the dance and stage coach at the YMCA's Camp Porter. In what used to be an American tradition, he worked his way through college, among the evening, weekend and vacation jobs he lists stacking tires in a warehouse, soda-jerking, ditch-digging and concrete-mixing, all in addition to entertainment engage-

James, Gene and Fred Kelly

Counselor Kelly at Camp Porter in the summer of 1931

11

ments with Fred, then considered the dancer of the family and the one most likely to make dancing his profession.

By his senior year at the University of Pittsburgh Gene Kelly was well known on campus as an entertainer in their *Cap and Gown* shows, and he was put in charge of directing the student company. After graduating in 1933 he went to law school for two months, but quit when he realized his appetite for dancing was now dominant in his thinking. A great factor in making this decision was his mother, who had maintained her interest in dancing and with a group of local parents had put together a kind of school, for which they hired a dancing teacher on the weekends. Mrs. Kelly had inveigled her son to assist the teacher, and she had also taken a job in a dancing school in order to learn the business side of it—and get free lessons for Fred. Mother and son Gene then founded a dancing school in the family basement: "I found I had a penchant for teaching, that I liked it and that I was good with children. This eventually led to choreography—and to be a good choreographer you must first be a good teacher, because you have to show people what to do and convince them they can do it. The man who changed the course of dancing, one of the first great choreographers, Michael Fokine, was before that a star dancer and you must be able to dance in order to teach. So much of it has to do with inspiring confidence. However, with time I became disenchanted with teaching because the ratio of girls to boys was more than ten to one, and once the girls reached sixteen the dropout rate was very high. They would lose interest, or get fat or gauche, or take up other lines. A dancer must be dedicated, yet that dedication can make girls tense and nervous. Many haven't the stamina to stay with it, and others have the dedication without the ability."

The family dance enterprise was quickly successful and soon moved from the basement to a hired hall. It was decided to call it *The Gene Kelly Studio of the Dance,* and the next year the farsighted Mrs. Kelly opened up a branch in Johnstown: "We had relatives there and they said they needed dancing lessons for their children. We organized a class in the Legion Hall, then a bigger hall, and finally it turned into a studio bigger than the one in Pittsburgh. We drew on all the mill communities around Johnstown and as the times improved and the mills opened up, we did very good business. My Fridays and Saturdays were

Louise and Gene in 1932

12

spent in Johnstown, and so it went for three years, with me all the time dreaming about one day being a great choreographer."

As a teacher Gene Kelly also sought tuition for himself, in order to be at least a step ahead of his pupils. He and Fred each summer attended the sessions of the Chicago National Association of Dancing Masters, where expert instructors gave advice on all manner of dances. Fred had already made the decision to dance for a living but Gene had loftier aims. "I read everything I could get my hands on about ballet and in Chicago I studied with Bernice Holmes, a lady who had the ability to teach men and she had learned her business from Adolph Bolm of the Diaghilev company."

To carry them through the summers in Chicago the Kelly brothers had to find work to pay for their lessons and their lodgings. They danced in an exhibition at the World's Fair but most of their jobs were far less impressive. As a pair of song-and-dance men doing numbers like "It's the Irish in Me," they played for small wages in sleazy nighteries. "I remember one in particular, a grubby joint out in the boondocks. An agent had sent us there to do two shows for five dollars, but the owner demanded four, and with a pair of bruisers at his side we weren't about to argue. It was 4:30 in the morning when we finished, and dawn by the time we got back into town. I went to the agent to complain, but all he did was demand his fifty cents commission. So I hit him—so hard I broke a finger in my hand, and had to spend the money getting it fixed in a hospital. I hadn't learned to control my temper—and I didn't really get to control it until years after I'd been in Hollywood."

In the summer of 1937 Gene Kelly went to New York with the object of finding work as a choreographer. Now twenty-five, his taste for the musical stage had been whetted by contact with many professionals. He had acquired a reputation as an advisor on improving song-and-dance material: "I had routined quite a lot of acts by now, for people coming through Pittsburgh on tour. They needed somewhere to rehearse and my studio came to their attention, and after a while I found myself known as a kind of dance-doctor. They would call on me to spruce up their dancing and occasionally I would get as much as a hundred dollars to devise a new routine. That was big money in those days." However, despite the feeling of affluence and the confidence borne of knowing people in the business, Kelly's rounds of the agents and the producers came to naught and he returned to Pitts-

The proprietor of The Gene Kelly School of the Dance in 1934

13

The director of the *Cap and Gown* show at the University of Pittsburgh, also in 1934

Lt. (j.g.) Gene Kelly, USN

Kelly, to the left of Mary Martin, and his comrades back up her famous debut singing "My Heart Belongs to Daddy" in *Leave It to Me* - Broadway, 1938

In New York in 1938 and the start of a career in show business

14

With Grace McDonald in
One For the Money - Broadway, 1939

With Vivienne Segal in *Pal Joey*

With Vivienne Segal in *Pal Joey*

With Shirley Paige in *Pal Joey*

burgh at the end of the summer to resume supervision of the dancing schools, now bringing the Kelly family an annual net income of eight thousand dollars.

Kelly's first extended job as a choreographer came in April of 1938, when he was hired by Charles Gaynor to help stage the musical revue *Hold Your Hats* at the Pittsburgh Playhouse, for which Gaynor wrote the sketches, the lyrics and the music. The show ran for a month, with Kelly appearing in six of the sketches and doing one solo, "La Cumparsita," which piece of music would be the basis of his elaborate Spanish number in MGM's *Anchors Aweigh* eight years later.

His applause in this revue encouraged Kelly to take another crack at Broadway. His timing, and his luck, were good. Robert Alton had been hired as the dance director of the Cole Porter musical *Leave It To Me,* which went into rehearsal in the late summer of 1938 and opened on Broadway at the Imperial Theatre on November 21. He invited Kelly to audition as a dancer. Still not having landed himself a position as a choreographer, he accepted and won a part. Alton and his wife had staged a show at the Pittsburgh Playhouse the previous Christmas, and they had been impressed with Kelly's work as a teacher. The Porter show was about an American ambassador, played by Victor Moore, who is sent to Russia against his preference for London and how a shrewd newspaperman, played by William Gaxton, helps him deliberately ruin his assignment in order to be recalled. Kelly played one of the ambassador's secretaries and in the fourth scene of the second act he and the other secretaries, all in fur parkas, backed up the newspaperman's stripper-girlfriend as she sang "My Heart Belongs to Daddy." Mary Martin, fresh from Texas, started her career with this saucy song, admitting years later that she then had little understanding of some of the Porter lines.

By the time *Leave It To Me* made its first appearance Robert Alton was already working on John Murray Anderson's revue *One for the Money,* with music by Morgan Lewis and sketches and lyrics by Nancy Hamilton. Kelly auditioned and won a leading part, requiring him to act, sing and dance in eight routines. The response to his work gave him reason to feel he had found his place in the scheme of things, and he had little trouble finding other jobs. He spent the summer of 1939 as a choreographer with the famed summer stock company of Westport, Connecticut, working on a revue and a musical treatment of O'Neill's *The Emperor Jones,* with Paul Robeson. The director of these shows, John Haggott, was employed by The Theatre Guild as a stage manager for its winter season; he had been responsible for Kelly's getting the job at Westport and he also arranged for him to audition for the Guild's presentation of William Saroyan's new play, *The Time of Your Life.* The actor playing the part of Harry, a hopeful hoofer, had been discharged after the Boston tryout and Kelly was given the role. It called for an actor with some style as a dancer and a dancer with the ability to build a character, this being the part of a rather sad man whose ambitions as a dancer will probably never come to be. Harry is one of a number of assorted, ordinary characters who loiter in a waterfront saloon in San Francisco. Kelly's hoofer gently danced his way through the show, giving the impression of im-provisation but actually doing the same routine every night. It was, in fact, dance-acting, and his first chance to perform in material of his own in-vention. *The Time of Your Life* was the real beginning of Kelly's career; it opened at the Booth Theatre on November 13, 1939, ran for twenty-two weeks and won a Pulitzer Prize.

The summer of 1939 saw Gene Kelly back at Westport, where he directed the dances for Lynn Riggs's play *Green Grow the Lilacs,* this being the vehicle that Rodgers and Hammerstein three years later turned into *Oklahoma!* Returning to New York at the close of the summer season, Kelly applied for the job of dance director for *Billy Rose's Diamond Horseshoe.* Recalls Kelly: "Rose was the hardest, toughest man I've ever met in this business, but I'm grateful to him because he was the man who gave me my first job as a choreog-rapher in New York. When I arrived at the audi-tion he was mean and rude and negative, so I swore at him in return. He said something like, "Don't you talk to me that way," and I replied I wouldn't want to work for him anyway. This amused him, so he invited me to sit and talk and tell him my ideas on the show. He liked this and offered me $115 a week. I said I wouldn't work for that, so he laughed again and added another twenty dollars." Also hired for this show was a seventeen-year-old dancer named Betsy Blair, whom Kelly shortly thereafter began to court. They were married on September 22, 1941 and their only child, a daughter named Kerry, was born on October 16, 1942. She is married and working as a child psychologist in London.

With wife Betsy Blair in 1944

The new movie star - Hollywood, 1942

After setting up the dances for *Billy Rose's Diamond Horseshoe* Kelly was called to audition for a musical comedy Rodgers and Hart had written with John O'Hara, *Pal Joey*. George Abbott was hired as director and Kelly's friend Robert Alton was brought in to direct the dancing. The musical play was a departure from standard Broadway musicals, being considerably more adult in its material and more subtle in the fusion of songs and dances with the characters and the situations. It called for a leading man of unusual ability, someone who could not only sing and dance but who could act well enough to create an ingratiating cad, a nightclub entertainer called Joey Evans, who makes his unscrupulous way through life using people, mainly women, and succeeding, never conscious of the pain he causes. *Pal Joey* opened at the Ethel Barrymore Theatre on December 25, ran for 270 performances, and made a star of Kelly. "It was a case of being the right man in the right place at the right time, and also a case of tremendous luck to have a part like that to play—to have a script by John O'Hara and songs by Rodgers and Hart, and a director like Abbott. I think I did well in it because it gave me a chance to use my own style of dancing to create a character. I wanted to dance to American music and at that time nobody else was doing it. And Joey was a meaty character to play. He was completely amoral. After some scenes I could feel the waves of hate coming from the audience. Then I'd smile at them and dance and it would relax them. It was interesting to be able to use the character to manipulate the audience."

In reviewing *Pal Joey* for *The New York Times*, John Martin wrote: "If Kelly were to be judged exclusively by his actual performance of the dance routines that fall to him, he would still be a good dancer, but when his dancing is seen in this fuller light he becomes an exceptional one. A tap dancer who can characterize his routines and turn them into an integral element of an imaginative theatrical whole would seem to be pretty close, indeed, to unique . . . he is not only glib-footed, but he has a feeling for comment and content that both gives his dancing personal distinction and raises it several notches as a theatre art."

At the time he was appearing in *Pal Joey* Kelly told interviewers, "I don't believe in conformity to any school of dancing. I create what the drama and the music demand. While I am a hundred percent for ballet technique, I use only what I can adapt to my own use. I never let technique get in the way of the mood or the continuity." That viewpoint appears not to have altered—it would seem, in fact, to have been his credo all through the years as a performer-choreographer in Hollywood. Backing up that attitude has been an inordinate capacity for hard work. Van Johnson had a small role in *Pal Joey* and he recalls: "I watched him rehearsing, and it seemed to me that there was no possible room for improvement. Yet he wasn't satisfied. It was midnight and we had been rehearsing since eight in the morning. I was making my way sleepily down the long flight of stairs when I heard staccato steps coming from the stage . . . I could see just a single lamp burning. Under it, a figure was dancing . . . Gene."

Gene Kelly believes that love of work is at least as important as possessing talent in order to succeed as an entertainer: "You have to love being in this business otherwise you couldn't stand it because it's so hard. It's almost masochistic and you couldn't do it if you didn't enjoy it. *The Loneliness of the Long-Distance Runner* could just as well be the story of a dancer, it's the same kind of effort. And you have to be born with a love of movement. As a boy I loved to run and jump—to move through the air and against the ground. You can't dance without that love."

Pal Joey is interesting to anyone studying the nature of the entertainment industry and its people. Says Kelly: "There are a lot of Pal Joeys in this business and perhaps a little of him in every man who has become a successful actor. There's a tendency to believe one's publicity and to forget the people who helped you. It's the kind of business that forces a man to be self-seeking, and it's childlike and narcissistic in many ways. Most male actors realize this after a while and look to do other things. The reason I escaped the problem early is that I didn't want to be an actor—I acted because I couldn't get a job as a choreographer or director, which is what I really wanted to do. I succeeded as an actor because I was a good dancer. The musical theatre needs male dancers all the time, and the fact that here was one who could say "hello" convincingly and carry a tune made it easy for me. I was never out of work in New York."

Hollywood offers began to arrive soon after *Pal Joey* was launched, but Kelly bided his time before accepting any. He finally signed a contract with David O. Selznick, agreeing to go to Hollywood in October of 1941, at the completion of his commitment to *Pal Joey* and after having done the choreography for the stage version of *Best Foot*

Forward. The problem with being signed to Selznick was that he produced very few films and had no interest in making musicals. He was convinced of Kelly's ability as an actor and prepared him to play the young priest in *The Keys of the Kingdom,* the part that was later played by Gregory Peck. Kelly finally talked Selznick out of the assignment but the great producer insisted on having him in the picture and asked him to take the part of the Scottish doctor. Kelly protested that his Scots accent was ridiculous but Selznick hired a dialect coach. "We worked together for a few weeks and then shot a scene. David and I looked at it, and then at each other—and began to laugh. I still sounded like a third-rate vaudevillian, so he wisely called in Thomas Mitchell to play the doctor. Selznick had nothing else on tap, so he sold fifty percent of my contract to MGM and loaned me to them to do *For Me and My Gal.*"

Kelly was not impressed with his debut in Hollywood: "They previewed the picture in Riverside and I was appalled at the sight of myself blown up twenty times. I had an awful feeling that I was a tremendous flop, but when I came outside executives started pumping my hand and Judy Garland came up and kissed me. I went home thinking they were just being nice, and I really didn't believe them until the picture opened in New York and did well. After that I wasn't sure how to handle all the things that quickly happened— the phone calls from newspapers and interviews for the radio. It was a new world and quite different from the theatre. In the theatre you can chug along for years, but being a success in the movies is like suddenly being turned into a rocket. Yet I still feel I'm better on the stage than on film."

MGM purchased the second half of Kelly's contract from Selznick, although there were a number of Metro executives who were not in favor of so doing. He was championed by Judy Garland and producer Arthur Freed, both of whom had seen him in *Pal Joey* and believed he had a future in film musicals. However, for his next assignment the studio used him purely as an actor in an inexpensive programmer, *Pilot No. 5,* followed by a filming of Cole Porter's *Du Barry Was a Lady,* minus most of the Porter songs. Kelly got his first chance at doing a self-choreographed dance in the all-star *Thousands Cheer* in which, as a soldier confined to barracks, he did a mock love-dance with a mop. His major impact as a persuasive, inventive dancer came when MGM loaned him to Columbia for *Cover Girl.* It was then apparent to the industry that Kelly had a unique quality to bring to films and in his next MGM musical, *Anchors Aweigh,* he was given almost *carte blanche* to devise several extensive routines, including the breakthrough in film choreography, the animated sequence with cartoon figures. It had taken him a couple of years, but Kelly had now hit his stride in Hollywood.

After completing his segment of *Ziegfeld Follies,* the famous dance-duet with Fred Astaire, Kelly left the studio for wartime service. At the end of 1944 he joined the United States Naval Air Service as an enlisted man and applied for a commission. After completing his training he was given the rank of lieutenant, junior grade. "I was in the Photographic Section, and they assumed I knew how to handle a camera, which I didn't. But I learned a lot about cameras the hard way, staying up nights. I was on my way to Japan when The Bomb dropped, and I didn't have to go. I was sweating that one out. You don't know how scared you can get when you ask for active duty and they finally give it to you."

Kelly was discharged from the navy in the spring of 1946; as an officer stationed at the photographic center in Washington, D.C. he had been responsible for writing and directing a number of documentaries, which had increased his interest in being involved in more production work when he returned to Hollywood. But MGM had nothing lined up for him and in looking around for a project they decided to use him in *Living in a Big Way,* a film so feeble that he was asked to devise musical sequences to interpolate afterwards. The film did little business but it drew the attention of the industry to Kelly's ability to create his own material. Believing that they were making a step forward in the maturing of the movie musical as a species, MGM gave Kelly, Judy Garland and Vincente Minnelli a fanciful yarn complete with an original Cole Porter score, *The Pirate.* Now regarded as a major achievement in the art of presenting songs and dances in an imaginative manner, the picture was given a poor reception by the general public. Fearing they had come up with something too sophisticated, MGM lost no time in putting both stars in more conventional and reliable formats.

But Gene Kelly was not content to appear in conventional and reliable movies, and kept hammering away at the management until he was given a film of his own to direct, one that was not at all conventional in its approach to telling a

On the set of *The Pirate* with visitor Irving Berlin

Rehearsing with Leonard Bernstein for *On the Town*

A pair of Von Stroheims. Stanley Donen and Kelly on the set of *On the Town* just prior to the first days' shooting

story in song and dance—*On the Town*. He shared the directing credit with Stanley Donen, whom he had brought to Hollywood shortly after his own arrival. Donen met Kelly when he arrived in New York at the age of eighteen and got a job in the chorus of *Pal Joey*. The two became friends, and Kelly gives Donen full credit as his invaluable assistant in most of his major movie musicals. Says Kelly: "To direct and be in front of the cameras at the same time is too hard, as I found out when I did my first picture without Stanley, *The Happy Road*. And when you are involved in doing choreography for film you must have expert assistants. I needed one to watch my performance, and one to work with the camerman on the timing, which is the most difficult part because cameramen are not musicians and a dancing sequence is all timing and movement. Without such people as Stanley, Carol Haney and Jeanne Coyne I could never have done these things. When we came to do *On the Town*, I knew it was time for Stanley to get screen credit because we weren't boss-and-assistant any more but co-creators, and in time he became a director in his own right."

The success of *On the Town* triggered off two fantastic years for Gene Kelly. By 1952 he was the star of the fabulous *An American in Paris* and the vastly amusing *Singin' in the Rain*, possibly the most popular of all movie musicals. He managed to develop the artistry of film choreography in a manner so apparently non-arty and so vital and appealing that the public was hardly aware of aesthetic pioneering. At all times in his films Kelly gave the appearance of being a likable, easygoing man but as John Green, his friend and head of music at MGM in this heyday period explains: "Gene is easygoing as long as you know exactly what you're doing when you're working with him. He's a hard taskmaster and he loves hard work. If you want to play on his team you'd better love hard work too. He isn't cruel but he is tough, and if Gene believed in something he didn't care who he was talking to, whether it was Louis B. Mayer or the gatekeeper. He wasn't awed by anybody and he had a good record of getting what he wanted. Gene's a survivor, and a good pupil of changing times."

Times changed for Kelly in the early fifties in a way that neither he nor his employers could have predicted. Television had made itself felt by this time and box-office earnings fell drastically. Most of the major studios either let go most of their stars or renegotiated their contracts in terms that

As a favor to director Stanley Donen, Kelly did a fleeting bit playing himself in *Love Is Better Than Ever* (1952). Here, leaving a Broadway restaurant, he stops to say hello to Larry Parks, playing a theatrical agent, while Elizabeth Taylor, as Parks' stagestruck girlfriend, looks on in awe.

With Maurice Chevalier in Paris in 1956, having hired the great entertainer to sing the title song for Kelly's *The Happy Road*

called for fewer commitments. Further, in releasing their libraries to television, the film producers created their own stiffest competition. Ironically, the film which suffered most was the musical, and by the end of the decade the original movie musical was veritably a thing of the past.

Despite his great popularity due to *Singin' in the Rain*, Kelly signed a contract with MGM in December of 1951 which sent him overseas for a period of nineteen months. It was signed for two major reasons—to allow MGM to take advantage of film funds frozen in Europe, with Kelly to make three pictures using those funds, and to allow him to qualify for income tax exemption under a new ruling stipulating that the earnings of Americans living abroad for a year and a half would be tax-free. While it seemed a feasible decision at the time, it backfired somewhat, in keeping Kelly away from Hollywood at a time when he might have benefited from staying. It also allowed him to produce his dream-project, the all-dancing film, *Invitation to the Dance*, which involved his time and efforts for far too long and resulted in box-office failure—a failure that did nothing to assuage the worries of MGM.

Invitation to the Dance was not released until 1956, four years after it first went into production in England. By that time Gene Kelly was a dissatisfied employee of a studio not at all sure of its future direction. MGM had several times refused

With assistant Jeanne Coyne and Sugar Ray Robinson, rehearsing the television show *Dancing - A Man's Game*

21

to loan Kelly to other studios—the last loan-out had been in 1944—but with their refusal to let Kelly play "Sky Masterson" in Sam Goldwyn's production of *Guys and Dolls,* the relationship between the star and the studio became strained. Goldwyn gave the role to Marlon Brando and, in a bitterly ironic move, turned over the film to MGM to distribute. Looking back on this period, Kelly commented: "I couldn't stand being inactive, it drove me almost berserk. They had cold feet about doing musicals and I was a song-and-dance man wondering what the hell I was going to do. Finally I asked for a settlement on the contract and we came to terms. I was to do two more films for them in addition to MGM coming in with me on a co-production of my own picture *The Happy Road.* This all worked out fairly well except that in severing myself from MGM I also cut myself off from the pension plan. Had I hung on a few years longer I believe I would have qualified for several thousands of dollars a year for life. But I just couldn't take sitting around with nothing to do."

After directing *The Tunnel of Love* and appearing in *Les Girls,* Kelly was clear of his contract with MGM. The sixteen-year association had been a glorious one for much of the time, and Kelly speaks well of his former employers: "It's become fashionable to sneer at the establishment and deride the old movie moguls but I don't go along with that. They were tough men and they mostly knew what they were doing. They made Hollywood the fifth largest industry in America. The mogul was a special breed—part tycoon and part artist, and we could use some of that breed even now. I admired their kind of toughness. They gave in to the talent more than you might think, and in the heyday of the Metro musical they scouted the country for the best dancers, writers, directors and musicians. For anyone connected with musicals it was Mecca. It's sad that it all had to come to an end but you can't blame the moguls for that."

Kellys first film after leaving MGM was *Marjorie Morningstar* for Warners. The picture met with mixed reviews, but some critics felt that it was his best dramatic work and assumed this would be the tone of his future in films. But Kelly was no longer interested in being a movie star; he wanted to devote his time to film production and accept whatever offers came his way for his services as an actor or director in any medium provided they were of sufficient interest.

Kelly's first job in this new phase of his career

was directing Rodgers and Hammerstein's new musical play *Flower Drum Song,* a considerable feather in his cap. Shortly after, still in New York, he devised, produced and performed in a television documentary for the prestigious NBC series, "Omnibus," calling it "Dancing—A Man's Game." Kelly here stated the case for his art in a no-nonsense manner. His appeal to the public has always rested on his image as a muscular, likable workingman, in no way highbrow or effete, and he is well aware of the stigma attached to male dancers: "There's a strong link between sports and dancing, and my own dancing springs from my early days as

an athlete. I played ice hockey as a boy and some of my steps come right out of that game—wide open and close to the ground. I think dancing is a man's game, and if a man does it well he does it better than a woman. Unfortunately, in the western world dancing is treated as a woman's game. This isn't so in the east. In Russia the dancer is a hero, and they can't understand why we make heroes of crooners. I don't want this to sound as if I'm against women dancing—we just have to remember that each sex is capable of doing things the other can't.

"Also, dancing *does* attract effeminate young men. I don't object to this as long as they don't dance effeminately. I know nothing about homosexuality, so I'm not qualified to discuss it. I only say that if a man dances effeminately he is dancing badly—just as if a woman comes out on the stage and starts to sing bass. It's wrong. As for the personal sexual tendencies, and their bearings on being a dancer, I think this has been overemphasized. This stigma on dancing is tragic because a great many boys would benefit from dancing lessons. It's the finest kind of exercise and it teaches poise. Unfortunately, people confuse gracefulness with softness. John Wayne is a graceful man and so are

With Claude Bessy, Helen Rae and Attilio Labis, rehearsing *Pas de Deux* at the Paris Opera House in 1960

many of the great ball players. A quarterback making a forward pass can be as beautiful as a ballet movement, and a double-play in baseball, if it's done well, has a choreographic feeling. Boxers, from James J. Corbett to Sugar Ray Robinson use dancing as part of their art but, of course, they don't run any risk of being called sissies. One of our problems is that so much dancing is taught by women. You can spot many male dancers who have this tuition by their arm movements—they're feminine and soft and limp. The main problem is that we badly need male dancers and so many young men who have talent are put off by the belief that it is an effeminate business. I like to think things have improved in recent years but I have no proof that they have."

Among the highlights in this latter stage of the Gene Kelly career is his staging of the first jazz ballet at the Paris Opera House. A Francophile and fluent in French, Kelly has been a hero to the French ever since *An American in Paris* and a cult-figure among French film makers because of his work in musicals. Early in 1960 he was invited by A. M. Julien, the general administrator of the Paris Opéra and Opéra-Comique to choose material of his own liking and invent a modern ballet for the company. The result was *Pas de Dieux*, combining a telling of Greek mythology with the music of George Gershwin's *Piano Concerto in F*. The story has Zeus coming to earth to win back his wife Aphrodite, who has taken up with the low life on the Left Bank. He manages to do this after the usual quota of problems. Kelly's major problem was in teaching the rigidly, classically trained corps de ballet how to relax their concepts and move in different ways. "It was like an athlete learning to ski after having spent years training to be a boxer. The jazz dancing required the use of different muscles, but they were willing subjects." *Pas de Dieux* was a conspicuous success, and at its opening night received twenty-two curtain calls. Where the French had formally liked Kelly, now they honored him, and his creation for the Paris Opera House was the major consideration in his being elected a Chevalier of the Legion of Honor by the French government.

It was in 1960 that Gene Kelly married for the second time. He and Betsy Blair separated in 1956 and were divorced the following year. The second Mrs. Kelly had known her husband for years prior to the marriage; Jeanne Coyne was a student at Kelly's dancing school in Pittsburgh when she was a teenager. Later she danced in musicals in New York and went to Hollywood in the late forties. She was a dancer in *The Pirate* and Kelly hired her as an assistant choreographer in 1949, thereafter working with him on all productions and retiring with their marriage. They have two children: Timothy, born March 3, 1962, and Bridget, born June 10, 1964.

Aside from a few appearances in films Kelly in the 1960s was engaged mostly in production work and in directing, occasionally with disappointing results. His directing of Jackie Gleason in *Gigot* in Paris was a particularly unhappy instance of a film's being so drastically cut and reedited by others that the intent of the original was spoiled. Another French endeavor, Jacques Demy's ambitious *hommage* to the MGM musical, *The Young Girls of Rochefort*, with Kelly as one of the stars, was too limp to make any impression.

Kelly was active on television throughout the decade, appearing on most of the major variety shows as a guest doing light dancing, "The heavy dancing is all behind me, but this mini-dancing on variety shows is fun and it helps me stay in shape." Among his major TV efforts were a special called "New York, New York" in 1966, and his direction and production of "Jack and the Beanstalk" in 1967, for which he won an Emmy.

Kelly's only fling at a TV series was a failure. He appeared in late 1962 as Father O'Malley in "Going My Way," in the role originated by Bing Crosby, but the timing was wrong. "I was hemmed in by the strict censorship then in effect, which allowed a Catholic priest to do nothing untoward. Our idea was that he be a two-fisted character and a social crusader, but the censors cut us down. It would have been interesting to have made the series years later when the medium and the public were more mature."

Gene Kelly was honored on November 18, 1969 when a tribute to him delivered by the Hon. Thomas M. Rees, Representative from California, was entered in the *Congressional Record*. The tribute saluted his contributions to the entertainment industry, but also mentioned that he had been cited by the government in 1945 and 1947 for services rendered and that he had traveled as a goodwill ambassador for the State Department in 1964.

But it is as a film dancer and choreographer that Kelly will be remembered, and especially for his development of screen dancing in a way that was acceptable to the mass public. "I belonged to the sweatshirt generation, and I felt uncomfortable

Being invested a Chevalier of the Legion of Honor at the Paris Opera House by director A.M. Julien

With daughter Kerry at the investiture of the Legion of Honor

At a Paris party in 1961 with another ex-M-G-M Kelly - Princess Grace, with Prince Rainier

With Nadia Westmore and Leo G. Carroll in the TV series *Going My Way*

With Bobby Riha in the television special *Jack and the Beanstalk*

in a tuxedo. I couldn't be another Fred Astaire and I had very little interest in doing *Swan Lake*. I grew up at a time when the American theatre was coming into its own and by the time I got to New York I knew I wanted to dance to American music, and try and find a style that could be called American. For me it was an extention of being a sports-oriented Pittsburgh kid. I wanted reality and vitality in addition to sophistication. I wasn't alone in this movement—people like Martha Graham and Humphrey Weidman were creating a whole new art form while I was struggling to find a style for myself. And by the time I found my style I got into films, and then found I was into something completely different from the stage and its dancing requirements. Dancing for the camera is comparatively very difficult."

The main difference between stage and screen dancing is one of perspective. Kelly explains: "On the stage you dance in the framework of the proscenium arch, the audience is in front of you and they see a three-dimensional image. They see with two eyes and they can absorb the environment. The one-eyed lens of the camera allows the audience to see only that portion of the scenery behind the dancer, and he becomes a two-dimensional figure. So you lose one of the most vital aspects of the dance—the sense of kinetic force, and the feeling of that third dimension. To compensate for that I put myself and my colleagues to thinking of dances that were purely cinematic—dancing with a cartoon, dancing with yourself in double exposure, dancing across interesting locations and being tracked by the camera. You have to construct a dance so it can be cut and edited, and do it in a way that won't disturb the viewer. You learn to use the camera as part of the choreography. It's possible that a lot of fine dancing has been ineffectual in the movies because it was never photographed imaginatively. Filming dancing will always be a problem because the eye of the camera is coldly realistic, demanding that everything looks natural, and dancing is unrealistic. That's the challenge, and all art is a compromise between your ideas and whatever means you have at your disposal."

There seems little likelihood that the movie musical will ever again become a staple of the cinema. The odds are all against it. The outlet for musical presentations will undoubtedly be television, ever improving in technical and artistic quality. Since 1960 most movie musicals have been filmed treatments of established stage vehicles, but

With wife Jeanne and their children Timothy and Bridget in the Kelly back garden on Bridget's third birthday, June 10, 1967

27

so many of them have been financial disasters that backers have come to regard the film musical as the worst of risks. The problems of costs and risks also apply to the wellspring of such films—the New York theatre, which in the 1960s produced an ever-diminishing number of successful musicals. This shortage is allied to the great changes in taste in popular music since the early fifties, with the accent of the music industry attuned to the younger generation. In the opinion of Gene Kelly: "This is a peculiar problem. Much of the youth-oriented music is admirable in its own right but hardly any of it lends itself to dramatic treatment. Many of the songs are charming, but they are not really for dancing. The authors of *Hair* came to see me about doing it as a film, but they had no script and you can't ad lib a movie musical. And the discotheque kind of dancing, this weird mixture of African tribal rites and the varsity drag, electrifying as it may be in person, means nothing when you put it on film. You need discipline and coordinated team work to make musicals—it's one area of filmmaking where the now popular *auteur* theory just does not make sense."

Gene Kelly, a hale and hearty sixty-one as this book goes to press, has long been considered one of the more solid citizens of Beverly Hills. He has lived in the same house since 1946 and prefers the conservative lifestyle, but is politically liberal and an active supporter of the Democrats. Nothing about Kelly smacks of the bizarre or the flamboyant, and his manner is more that of a successful, dignified business executive than that of a movie star. However, this demeanor is somewhat at variance with his feelings for the business world. "I have little talent for business. Actually the only thing I don't get a kick out of in show business is 'business.' But I still feel it's fun to act, fun to direct, fun to dance, fun to do all the things one does either in front of or behind the camera. And I'll continue to participate whenever and however fortune dictates."

In reviewing his career Kelly expresses no serious regrets: "I think I would like to have made a picture with Cary Grant or a western with John Ford but I've been very fortunate in doing most of the things I wanted to do. I'd like to make a few more movies, mainly as a director, and I have a notion to direct something entirely different from what I've done before, perhaps a Shakespearean tragedy. But even if it never comes to be, I have no cause to complain. A career came my way —I didn't set out in pursuit of one. I took it as it came, and it turned out to be very nice. A man can hardly be luckier than that."

With French director Jacques Demy while making *The Young Girls of Rochefort*

With Adolph Zukor on his 100th birthday - January 7, 1973

THE FILMS

With Judy Garland

FOR ME AND MY GAL

CREDITS:

An MGM Production 1942. Produced by Arthur Freed. Directed by Busby Berkeley. Screenplay by Richard Sherman, Fred Finklehoffe and Sid Silvers. Based on a story by Howard Emmett Rogers. Photographed by William Daniels. Art direction by Cedric Gibbons. Edited by Ben Lewis. Dances directed by Bobby Connolly. Music direction by George Stoll. Running time: 100 minutes.

CAST:

Jo Hayden: Judy Garland; *Harry Palmer:* Gene Kelly; *Red Metcalfe:* George Murphy; *Eve Minard:* Marta Eggerth; *Sid Sims:* Ben Blue; *Lily Duncan:* Lucille Norman; *Danny Duncan:* Richard Quine; *Eddie Miller:* Kennan Wynn; *Bert Waring:* Horace McNally.

The difficulty of playing a leading role in his first film was somewhat eased for Gene Kelly by the nature of the material. *For Me and My Gal* required him to play a charming, but conceited and selfish young song-and-dance man, a part not greatly removed from the characterization of *Pal Joey.* The songs and dances themselves were all familiar ones—at least familiar to anyone with knowledge of the American entertainment business in the years of the First World War, the milieu of the film. In Busby Berkeley Kelly had a director who knew this kind of story from personal experience. Berkeley had served in the U.S. Army in France and had started his career staging shows for the troops. Says Kelly, "I knew nothing about filming when we started and I was scared, but by the time we finished I had picked up quite a lot of know-how, thanks to Berkeley and thanks to Judy, who had a lot to do with persuading MGM to use me in the picture."

For Me and My Gal opens in a little town in Ohio; a troupe of entertainers arrive to play the local theatre, among them Jo Hayden (Judy Garland, Red Metcalfe (George Murphy), Lily Duncan (Lucille Norman) and Sid Sims (Ben Blue), a quartet of singer-dancers who travel the vaudeville circuit. Also in the company is a breezy hoofer, Harry Palmer (Kelly), who makes up to Jo and persuades her they will be a good team, and that they should set their sights on the Palace Theatre in New York, the high spot of the vaudeville circuit. She becomes his partner and gradually falls in love with him, a feeling the ambitious Harry fails either to recognize or reciprocate. He falls under the spell of singing star Eve Minard (Marta Eggerth) and the romance shows every sign of helping his career. Although Jo and Harry have been together for two years they still have not reached the top of the business, and realizing how much he wants to get there, the unselfish Jo goes to Eve and asks her to help him. This she is prepared to do, but when Harry hears about it he has a change of heart; he realizes his own love for Jo and decides to stick with her.

Eventually Jo and Harry receive an offer from the Palace but when they get to the theatre in New York they learn there has been an error—the booking should have made clear it was the Palace Theatre in Newark. They do their act in Newark and do it so well they get an offer of a contract for the big Palace but in the midst of their celebrations Harry receives his draft call to join the army. Determined to let nothing stand in the way of his career, Harry smashes his hand in a trunk and sustains a injury sufficient to get him a deferment. His timing turns out to be bad; Jo learns of his cowardly ruse just as she learns that her young brother has been killed on active duty in France, and she walks out on Harry.

A contrite Harry tries to make amends by enlisting but he is turned down. He then joins a YMCA entertainment unit, along with Sid Sims, and they are shipped to France. He finds that Jo is traveling around the battle areas entertaining the troops, and in order to vindicate himself in her eyes he performs an act of heroism. The lovers are united and with the signing of the armistice they resume their career, which takes them to the Palace in New York.

The plot of *For Me and My Gal* is banal and frequently maudlin, but it is generously laced with musical numbers and the performances are altogether pleasing if not striking. It is really Judy

With George Murphy and Judy Garland

With George Murphy, Lucille Norman and Judy Garland

With Judy Garland

Garland's picture—it was, in fact, her first solo billing—and Kelly is a little bland as the cocky cad, although his performance was sufficient to win him approval as a "likable new find" wherever the picture played. The part of Harry was originally slated for George Murphy but pressure from Arthur Freed and Judy Garland got Kelly the job, with Murphy then taking the next-best role as the faithful friend of the heroine—the nice guy who doesn't get the girl.

The score of the film includes eighteen songs and dances; the title song and "When You Wore a Tulip" are sung by Garland and Kelly as duets, and they also perform the classic jazz-dance "Ballin' the Jack." Kelly does the solo "Tramp Dance," and with Ben Blue he does the vaudeville ditty, "Frenchie, Frenchie." Garland has several extended solos—"Oh, You Beautiful Doll," "Smiles," "Till We Meet Again," and "After You've Gone"— but much of her footage is spoiled by Berkeley's exceedingly sentimental direction. *For Me and My Gal* is very old-fashioned entertainment and now comes within the boundaries of what is vaguely known as "camp."

Gene Kelly looks back on the filming as an exciting but uncomfortable period: "I still feel more at ease on a stage than I do before the cameras but at that time I was constantly thrown by the piecemeal way pictures are made. I knew nothing about playing to the camera, and I didn't know whether I was being shot close, medium or long, or about the intricate business of hitting all the marks laid out on the studio floor for the movements of the actors. It was Judy who pulled me through. She was very kind and helpful, and more helpful than she even realized because I watched her to find out what I had to do. Judy was only twenty, but she had been in pictures for six years. I was amazed at her skill; she knew every mark and every move. All I could do for her then was help with the dancing. She wasn't a dancer, but she could pick up a step instantly, and as a singer she was incredible—she had only to hear a melody once and it was locked in her mind. I learned a great deal about making movies doing this first one, and much of it was due to Judy Garland."

With Martha Eggerth

With George Murphy, Judy Garland, Ben Blue and Keenan Wynn

With Judy Garland

32

With Ben Blue

With Addison Richards and Ben Blue

With Judy Garland

With Marsha Hunt and Franchot Tone

PILOT NO. 5

CREDITS:

An MGM Production 1943. Produced by B. P. Fineman. Directed by George Sidney. Screenplay by David Hertz. Photographed by Paul C. Vogel. Art direction by Cedric Gibbons and Howard Campbell. Edited by George White. Musical score by Lennie Hayton. Running time: 70 minutes.

CAST:

George Braynor Collins: Franchot Tone; *Freddie:* Marsha Hunt; *Vito S. Alessandro:* Gene Kelly; *Everett Arnold:* Van Johnson; *Winston Davis:* Alan Baxter; *Henry Willoughy Claven:* Dick Simmons; *Major Eichel:* Steve Geray; *Hank Durban:* Howard Freeman; *Nikola:* Frank Puglia; *American Soldier:* William Tannen.

For his second film Gene Kelly opted for a straight dramatic story with no songs and dances, eager to prove his interest in being known as an actor as well as a musical performer. The film was made under the title *Skyway to Glory*, but MGM wisely decided against that pretentious label and chose to release it as *Pilot No. 5*, an uninspired choice that did nothing to draw the public. It was then shown as a "programmer"—something between an A and a B film, to be used as either top or bottom of a double bill depending on location and the studio's investment in the companion feature.

The story begins in March of 1942, at a bomb-blasted air base in Java, where a group of Allied survivors must decide what course to take in the face of the oncoming Japanese forces. The senior officer is a Dutch major, who finds he has five

34

With Marsha Hunt

With Marsha Hunt and Franchot Tone

With Dick Simmons, Steve Geray, Alan Baxter and Van Johnson

With Howard Freeman, Dick French,
Marsha Hunt and Franchot Tone

American pilots at his disposal but only one aircraft fit for service. The decision is made to use the plane, a fighter, to attack the Japanese in what will probably be a suicidal mission. The major calls for a volunteer and when all five men offer to make the flight he decides to choose the man who has the most logical plan of attack. The winner is George Collins (Franchot Tone), and after he has taken off the major wonders about him, about his character and background. Three of the pilots are acquainted with Collins and their recollections are depicted in flashback sequences which form most of the footage of *Pilot No. 5*.

The divergent opinions about Collins confuse the Dutch officer. Lt. Winston Davis (Alan Baxter) tells how, as an enlistment officer, he was hesitant about accepting Collins's application to join the Air Corps because of an unsavory reputation. Lt. Everett Arnold (Van Johnson) gives a better picture of the man remembered from school days as a law student, eager to succeed because of his love for Freddie (Marsha Hunt). The bulk of the story is learned, somewhat reluctantly, from Lt. Vito Alessandro (Gene Kelly), a former partner of Collins in the employ of a powerful but crooked state governor, Hank Durban (Howard Freeman). Alessandro reveals how the ambitious Collins went along with the venal politician until he himself quit in disgust. Eventually Collins followed suit, with his reputation subsequently blackened by the governor, and his spirit broken by the collapse of his career and the false belief that Alessandro had stolen the affections of Freddie, a lie fostered by Durban. Collins gradually regains respect when he fights back and exposes the governor. As Alessandro ends his story, radio reception from Collins informs them he is about to crash-dive his plane on a Japanese aircraft carrier.

The performance of Kelly as a moody Italian-American surprised those who had little reason to consider him an actor on the basis of his work in *Me and My Gal*. Slight though *Pilot No. 5* was, it proved that Kelly was not merely a visiting Broadway performer and that he obviously had a future in films. As Kelly recalls: "The picture started out to be something bigger and stronger than it finally emerged. The original idea was a statement against fascism, to draw a parallel between the malpractice of political power in America and the kinds of fascism that had drawn America into the war. It was a warning against incipient fascism, somewhat based on Huey Long and the danger of one man's gaining control of a state. But the studio shied away from taking that kind of stand at that time, which isn't hard to understand—we were in the entertainment business and this was wartime. So the script was defanged."

With Marsha Hunt

With Marsha Hunt and Franchot Tone

DU BARRY WAS A LADY

CREDITS:

An MGM Production 1943. Produced by Arthur Freed. Directed by Roy del Ruth. Screenplay by Irving Brecher, adapted by Nancy Hamilton from the musical play by Herbert Fields and B. G. DeSylva. Songs by Cole Porter, Lew Brown, Ralph Freed, Burton Lane, Roger Edens and E. Y. Harburg. Musical direction by George Stoll. Photographed in Technicolor by Karl Freund. Art direction by Cedric Gibbons. Edited by Blanche Sewell. Running time: 96 minutes.

CAST:

Louis Blore, King Louis: Red Skelton; *May Daly, Madame Du Barry:* Lucille Ball; *Alec Howe, Black Arrow:* Gene Kelly; *Ginny:* Virginia O'Brien; *Charlie, Dauphin:* Rags Ragland; *Rami,* *the Swami, Taliostra:* Zero Mostel; *Mr. Jones, Duc de Choiseul:* Donald Meek; *Willie, Duc de Rigor:* Douglas Dumbrille; *Cheezy, Count de Roquefort:* George Givot; *Niagara:* Louise Beavers; *and Tommy Dorsey and his Orchestra.*

Cole Porter's *Du Barry Was a Lady* suffered the same fate that every stage musical suffered when bought by a Hollywood studio in those years when the studios were all-powerful—the script was thoroughly rewritten, most of the songs were dropped and new ones added. The Porter show, which opened on Broadway in December of 1939, was a smash hit with Ethel Merman and Bert Lahr, but neither was considered strong enough with the moviegoing public to risk using in the film version. In the film their parts were played by Red Skelton and Lucille Ball, with the second

With Red Skelton and Lucille Ball

With Lucille Ball and Red Skelton

With Zero Mostel

leads, those played on Broadway by Ronald Graham and Betty Grable, going to Gene Kelly and Virginia O'Brien. Grable was then under contract to 20th Century-Fox and though they were agreeable to her playing on Broadway, they felt differently about her appearing in a Metro musical. The script of the Porter original was considered quite racy and spicy at the time, and the tone was much softened for the film; whereas the character played by Lahr on stage was a washroom attendant he was played as a cloakroom clerk by Skelton. The twenty songs written by Porter for the original were whittled down to three, and six new ones were written by Lew Brown, Ralph Freed, Burton Lane, E. Y. Harburg and Roger Edens.

Much of the film is set in the period of King Louis XIV with all of that footage in the form of a dream sequence. A hat-check boy, Louis Blore (Red Skelton), in a swank nightclub, is deeply in love with glib showgirl May Daly (Lucille Ball), who disdains to pay him attention—until he wins $75,000 in the Irish Sweepstake. She then becomes his fiancee, to the disappointment of song-and-dance man Alec Howe (Kelly). Due to his good fortune Louis is dubbed "King Louis" by newspapermen, and to further impress his bride-to-be he buys the nightclub. Alec's friend, Swami the Rami (Zero Mostel), a comic seer, predicts May will never marry Louis, and Louis, afraid that Alec may cause trouble at the engagement party, slips a drug into Alec's drink to render him unconscious. But it is Louis who downs the drink, causing him to fall sleep—and dream. The dream transports Louis and his friends back two hundred years, with Louis as the King, May as Du Barry and Alec as a dashing revolutionary leader known as The Black Arrow.

The situations in the dream reveal the same doubts Louis had in his real situation, with Du Barry showing the King little interest. He finds himself the intended victim of a plot, contrived by several of his courtiers and led by The Black Arrow. After a chain of ludicrous circumstances King Louis finds himself among the very crowd marching on the palace to kill him. He manages to gain control of the situation and sentences The Black Arrow to the guillotine, but Du Barry pleads for the life of the handsome rebel—for obvious reasons—promising Louis she will do anything for him in return. The King then tries to stop the execution but his cries are lost in the cries of the mob, and as The Black Arrow kneels under the knife, the dream fades and Louis wakes up in the nightclub, being attended by his friends. Taking the dream as a lesson and a warning, Louis comes to his senses about May and calls off his engagement. He promotes the engagement of May and Alec and realizes he loves Ginny, the club's cigarette girl, who has loved him all along.

Du Barry Was a Lady did good business at the box office, but was far from the blockbuster MGM had hoped for. Robbed of the sauciness of the stage original and the brilliant comic performance of Bert Lahr, the film's devices seem limp. Skelton and Lucille Ball are amusing, but only suggestive of the comic experts they would later become. More memorable are the smaller parts—Zero Mostel at the age of twenty-eight and making his film debut; Rags Ragland, whose death in 1946 cut short a thriving comic career, as a nightclub flunky who becomes the Dauphin of France in the dream sequence; and the deadpan chanteuse Virginia O'Brien singing a song about sex, "No Matter How Thin You Slice It, It's Still Salome."

Gene Kelly's role called for no great effort on his part, dance-romancing Lucille Ball and doing a lively group dance with beautiful chorus girls in the nightclub. His swashbuckling as The Black Arrow was a sign of things to come, and he was involved in the only two lasting songs from the film—both from Porter's original score—the ballad "Do I Love You, Do I?" and the catchy "Friendship," sung as the finale by all the main characters.

With Zero Mostel and Red Skelton

With Lucille Ball, Red Skelton, Virginia O'Brien and Tommy Dorsey

The Mop Dance

THOUSANDS CHEER

CREDITS:

An MGM Production 1943. Produced by Joe Pasternak. Directed by George Sidney. Screenplay by Paul Jarrico and Richard Collins. Photographed in Technicolor by George Folsey. Art direction by Cedric Gibbons. Edited by George Boemler. Musical direction by Herbert Stothart. Running time: 125 minutes.

CAST:

Kathryn Jones: Kathryn Grayson; *Eddy Marsh:* Gene Kelly; *Hyllary Jones:* Mary Astor; *Col. William Jones:* John Boles; *Chuck Polansky:* Ben Blue; *Marie Corbino:* Frances Rafferty; *Helen:* Mary Elliott; *Sergeant Kozlack:* Frank Jenks; *Alan:* Frank Sully; *Capt. Fred Avery:* Dick Simmons; *Private Monks:* Ben Lessy.

GUEST STARS: Mickey Rooney, Judy Garland, Red Skelton, Eleanor Powell, Ann Sothern, Lucille Ball, Virginia O'Brien, Frank Morgan, Lena Horne, Marsha Hunt, Marilyn Maxwell, Donna Reed, Margaret O'Brien, June Allyson, Gloria de Haven, John Conte, Sara Haden, Jose Iturbi, Don Loper and Maxine Barrat, and the bands of Kay Kyser, Bob Crosby and Benny Carter.

Thousands Cheer holds especial interest for film students because it is a prime example of a Hollywood product never likely to be produced again. These glittering all-star packages were purportedly made in the national interest as morale boosters in wartime and they were made at a time when the film studios were at the peak of their affluence and creativity. The rich resources of MGM and its talent roster were available to producer Joe Pasternak to make this film, and con-

With Ben Blue

With Ben Blue and Kathryn Grayson

temporary producers might well look with envy at what Pasternak then had at his disposal. The plot was thin, but musical numbers and sketches by twenty guest stars pumped it up to a pleasing two hours. The working title was *Private Miss Jones,* but this was dropped after the completion of the film in favor of *Thousands Cheer,* thereby causing some confusion with Irving Berlin's stage musical *As Thousands Cheer,* to which it bore no resemblance.

Much of the action of the story takes place at an army camp, where Kathryn Jones (Kathryn Grayson) gives up her career as a concert singer in favor of keeping house for her father, Col. William Jones (John Boles), long separated from his wife, Hyllary (Mary Astor). At a railway station, Private Eddie March (Kelly) spots Kathryn and despite his being a stranger, he kisses her because he is alone and feels the urge to kiss somebody goodbye. He is unaware that she is the daughter of the commandant of the camp for which he is bound, and when he later discovers this he is resentful because to him the girl represents military authority, which he hates. Eddie is a trapeze artist, a daring and successful aerialist and he has been drafted much against his wishes. He is conceited in his manner, and rude to Kathryn, until he is advised by his buddies to play up to her if he wants to make his desired transfer to the Air Corps. The idea backfires when Eddie finds himself in love with Kathryn and she with him. The colonel is alarmed at the affair and asks for the advice of his estranged wife. Meanwhile Eddie has taken Kathryn

With Kathryn Grayson and John Boles

41

With Kathryn Grayson and Mary Astor

With Will Kaufmann, Kathryn Grayson, Mary Elliot
and Frances Rafferty

to meet his circus family, the Corbinos, and she
discovers he was, in fact, the star of the act.

Eddie is worried when Kathryn's mother appears
on the scene, bound to persuade the girl to return
with her to New York. Kathryn begs for more time
because she is producing a camp show, to which
she has invited various famous entertainers, including Jose Iturbi. Eddie, by now a model soldier,
panics when he learns of the arrival of her mother,
deserts his guard post and barges into the colonel's
office to plead his case, which results in his being
confined to barracks. The day of the show arrives
and among the talent are The Corbinos, who
manage to persuade the colonel to release Eddie
in order to perform with them. His family understands Eddie's problems in adjusting to discipline
and cooperation, and while performing their high-
flying act they graphically impress upon him the
need for teamwork and reliance on others. After
the show, Hyllary is about to discuss her plans
for taking Kathryn away when the camp receives
its orders to proceed overseas. At the fadeout,
mother and daughter wave goodbye to the colonel
and his future son-in-law.

Hollywood was unstinting in its wartime efforts
to entertain the armed forces, sending units to
every camp on every front, but it's doubtful if any
camp received the kind of lavish show staged for
the troops in *Thousands Cheer*. One of the plot devices in the film is for the heroine to be a friend
of the Spanish concert pianist Jose Iturbi, who
here made the first of what would be several appearances in MGM musicals, helping to popularize
classical music and occasionally "letting his hair
down" with pop pieces. In this picture Iturbi has
a fling at boogie-woogie and accompanies Judy
Garland in a raucous, and now terribly dated,
song called "The Joint is Really Jumping Down
at Carnegie Hall," written by Roger Edens. Standing the test of time far better is Lena Horne with
"Honeysuckle Rose." The camp show has Mickey
Rooney as the master of ceremonies and aside
from introducing a raft of sketches he does his
impersonation of Clark Gable. Among the better
sketches are Red Skelton as a soda-jerk with a
weak stomach, made bilious by the appetite of
Margaret O'Brien for ice cream, and Frank Morgan as a fake navy doctor delighting over the
prospect of examining WAVE inductees Lucille
Ball and Ann Sothern. A variety of dance bands
play typical songs of the day like "I Dug a Ditch
and Struck it Rich in Wichita," and "Let There
be Music." Kathryn Grayson is heard to advantage

in an aria from *La Traviata,* and a song called "Daybreak," based on a melody by Ferde Grofe, with lyrics by Harold Adamson. The huge finale is "The United Nations Hymn," sung by Grayson and an army orchestra under Iturbi.

Despite the generous amounts of music in *Thousands Cheer,* Gene Kelly appears in only one sequence calling for dancing. As the private confined to barracks and ordered to clean the floor, he makes the job lighter by imagining his mop to be a girl. He glides around the floor waltzing to the tune "Let Me Call You Sweetheart," gradually making the dance more complex. At one point he aims the mop at a picture of Hitler and rat-a-tat-tats with his heel like a machine gun. Kelly's work in the picture was a clear step up in MGM's plan to register him with the public, and he was well received by most of the critics. In his review for The *New York Herald Tribune* Howard Barnes went so far to say Kelly dominated the film and "saves the picture from being merely a parade of personalities."

With Frances Rafferty and Mary Elliot

With Kathryn Grayson

43

THE CROSS OF LORRAINE

CREDITS:

An MGM Production 1943. Produced by Edwin Knopf. Directed by Tay Garnett. Screenplay by Michael Kanin, Ring Lardner, Jr., Alexander Eskay and Robert D. Andrews, based on a story by Lilo Damert and Robert Aisner and *A Thousand Shall Fall* by Hans Habe. Photographed by Sidney Wagner. Art direction by Cedric Gibbons and Daniel Cathcart. Edited by Dan Miller. Musical score by Bronislau Kaper. Running time: 89 minutes.

CAST:

Paul: Jean-Pierre Aumont; *Victor:* Gene Kelly; *Father Sebastian:* Sir Cedric Hardwicke; *Francois:* Richard Whorf; *Rodriguez:* Joseph Calleia; *Sergeant Berger:* Peter Lorre; *Duval:* Hume Cronyn; *Louis:* Billy Roy; *Major Bruhl:* Tonio Stewart; *Jacques:* Jack Lambert; *Pierre:* Wallace Ford; *Marcel:* Donald Curtis; *Rene:* Jack Edwards, Jr.; *Lt. Schmidt:* Richard Ryen.

The majority of Hollywood movies made during the years of the Second World War, dealing with that war, appear ludicrous when viewed a generation later. It can hardly be otherwise. This was entertainment with an intentional propagandistic purpose, and those films which dealt with the German occupation of various European countries suffer most in the time gap. *The Cross of Lorraine* is a case in point; despite its production values and some fine performances the unrelieved depiction of all Germans as vicious brutes and most Frenchmen as noble heroes robs it of any credibility. However, credit must be given the Hollywood studios for following through on requests

44

from Washington for pictures of this nature. MGM was asked to make *The Cross of Lorraine* to inculcate a better regard for France among the Allies.

It is, basically, a prison picture and like others of this genre it quickly sets up the backgrounds of a group of main characters, all of whom join the French army at the outbreak of the war and all of whom are captured when the French government capitulates. Chief among them are a promising Parisian lawyer, Paul (Jean-Pierre Aumont), a taxi driver with a scrappy nature, Victor (Gene Kelly), and Rodriguez (Joseph Calleia), a Spanish Republican intent on carrying on the fight against oppression. The film is little else but an indictment of German ruthlessness. The soldiers find themselves tricked—instead of being returned to their homes they are herded into railway boxcars and shipped off to a camp behind the German lines, there to be indoctrinated into belief in the New Order, a process that hardly seems feasible in view of the brutality meted out to them. A priest, Father Sebastian (Sir Cedric Hardwicke) is one of the captives and he is treated no better than the others —the heathen Huns even deny him the right to hold services. A nasty little German sergeant (Peter Lorre in one of his less memorable roles) steals from the prisoners, and a weasellike Frenchman, Duval (Hume Cronyn) makes use of his knowledge of the German language and decides to work for his captors.

Victor suffers torture and humiliation because of his belligerent attitude. At the initial interrogation he gives a weak Nazi salute and asks, "Heil, er, what's his name?" at which he is knocked unconscious and thrown into solitary confinement, where his spirit is sapped. The French soldiers find their plight little different from the inmates of concentration camps, with near-starvation, sickness, beatings and the idea of escape their sustaining force. Duval meets his due fate when the inmates put him on trial, find him guilty and then push him out into the night to be shot by the guards. Father Sebastian dies when he defies the Germans and holds a burial service—they shoot him as he intones the rites. Meanwhile, Paul assumes Duval's place, feigning loyalty to the Germans in order to facilitate the escapes of his comrades.

Paul arranges the escape of the ailing Victor; he substitutes him for a wounded German soldier, whose head is completely bandaged, and tricks the sergeant into letting him drive the soldier for badly needed attention at a nearby hospital. The sergeant accompanies Paul in the ambulance but he is dumped out and the two Frenchmen makes their way on foot until they are picked up by the French underground forces, who lead them to a village in a less densely occupied part of France. But while Paul and Victor are recuperating, a German army unit arrives in the village to recruit men for labor battalions. They make a show

With Billy Roy, Wallace Ford, Jean Pierre Aumont and Jack Lambert

of requesting volunteers but they clearly mean to arrest the required number of men. As the German officer addresses the crowd, Paul walks to the front to seemingly offer himself as a model volunteer but he then turns and incites the populace into revolt, which act costs him his life. At this, Victor snaps out of the defeatist stupor into which he had fallen and leads the villagers in a pitched battle to wipe out the German soldiers. With this accomplished, they burn the village to prevent its usefulness to other German units and march away to join the Resistance.

The Cross of Lorraine, with the flag of the Free French fluttering in the credit titles and numerous paraphrases of "La Marseillaise" in Bronislau Kaper's score, probably drew the political response it sought, provided it was paired with something more entertaining on a double bill. It also provided Gene Kelly with his most dramatic role in films, one which brought him good notices and one he considers among his best performances.

With Peter Lorre

With Richard Whorf and Jean Pierre Aumont

With Jean Pierre Aumont and Sir Cedric Hardwick

46

With Jean Pierre Aumont, Jack Lambert, Wallace Ford and Joseph Calleia

With Sir Cedric Hardwick and Joseph Calleia

With Jean Pierre Aumont and Richard Whorf

With Rita Hayworth

COVER GIRL

CREDITS:

A Columbia Production 1944. Produced by Arthur Schwartz. Directed by Charles Vidor. Screenplay by Virginia Van Upp, adapted by Marion Parsonnet and Paul Gangelin from a story by Erwin Gelsey. Photographed in Technicolor by Rudolph Maté and Allen M. Davey. Art direction by Lionel Banks and Cary Odell. Edited by Viola Lawrence. Songs by Jerome Kern and Ira Gershwin. Musical direction by Morris W. Stoloff. Running time: 107 minutes.

CAST:

Rusty Parker: Rita Hayworth; *Danny McGuire:* Gene Kelly; *Noel Wheaton:* Lee Bowman; *Genius:* Phil Silvers; *Jinx:* Jinx Falkenburg; *Maurine*

Martin: Leslie Brooks; *Cornelia Jackson:* Eve Arden; *John Coudair:* Otto Kruger; *John Coudair (as a young man):* Jess Barker; *Anita:* Anita Colby; *Chef:* Curt Bois; *Joe:* Ed Brophy; *Tony Pastor:* Thurston Hall.

In the history of the Hollywood musical *Cover Girl* marks a major turning point, a transitional point at which the long-familiar concept of the movie musical as a string of songs strung together by a skimpy plot gave way to a broader concept in which the musical sequences would form part of the plot. However, the plot of *Cover Girl* is paper-thin and in direct line with the many corny backstage musicals stretching back over the previous dozen years. Its value lies in the quality of the songs supplied by Jerome Kern and Ira Gershwin and how those songs are sung and danced. The film also marks a turning point in the career of

With Phil Silvers

With Phil Silvers and Rita Hayworth

Gene Kelly; until now he had been well received by the public as a pleasant entertainer with an obvious talent for dancing, but with *Cover Girl* it was apparent that he was not merely a dancer. It was here that Kelly made it known to both the public and the industry that he was capable of imaginative choreography of a purely cinematic kind, and equally capable of performing the highly complex and athletic dancing that choreography required.

Much of the story is set in a small Brooklyn nightclub owned by Danny McGuire (Kelly). One of his dancing girls, Rusty Parker (Rita Hayworth), with whom he also happens to be in love, attracts the attention of a magazine editor, John Coudair (Otto Kruger) when that magazine conducts a search for cover girls. His choice of Rusty is influenced by the fact that she is the granddaughter of the young lady he loved and lost when he was a young man. This story twist allows for an elaborate flashback sequence in which Hayworth is seen as the lady in question, a star of Tony Pastor's musical theatre. In this sequence she sings "Sure Thing" against a racetrack backdrop, and the lyrics draw a parallel between betting on horses and being lucky in love.

Danny, Rusty and the club's comic, known as Genius (Phil Silvers), are all show-biz hopefuls, a fact that is clearly stated in one of the film's most memorable segments; after a good night's work they close the club and cavort along a Brooklyn street singing a breezy song of optimism, "Make Way for Tomorrow," leaping over various objects, running up and down stairways, and giving merry

With Rita Hayworth

With Eve Arden, Otto Kruger, Rita Hayworth and Lee Bown

With Rita Hayworth

greetings to whomever comes their way. In total contrast, the film contains another street dance, Kelly's moody "Alter Ego" dance, in which he expresses his fears over the possible loss of his girlfriend. This fear proves groundless; after the ups and downs of the story have allowed for the presentation of several elaborate musical sequences, Rusty makes the decision to stay with Danny and not pursue a career.

The seven Kern-Gershwin songs all perform plot functions. The title song is used in the lavish staging of a cover-girl contest, and for this number Columbia recruited fifteen actual winners of magazine contests. The song "The Show Must Go On" is used in the nightclub in a simple, obvious manner, and Phil Silvers has a solo number, "Who's Complaining?" a topical ditty about rationing and wartime shortages. "Put Me to the Test" is a challenging love song for Kelly to express his feelings for Hayworth; the song begins in a dress shop and Kelly first tries out the lyrics on a dummy before later summoning up the courage to put them directly to his girl. The major song of the picture, the one which Ira Gershwin claims was the easiest to write, is the enduring "Long Ago and Far Away," which was also written for Kelly to sing to Hayworth. The setting is the nightclub after the close of business, with Kelly putting up chairs on tables as Silvers tinkles on the piano. Kelly is sad as he worries about his girl, but then

50

With Rita Hayworth

With Rita Hayworth, Phil Silvers and Ed Brophy

With Rita Hayworth and Phil Silvers

51

she comes onto the scene and he realizes she is his. The beautiful song then becomes the basis of an elegant, sensuous dance, and in this performance Kelly and Hayworth come close to matching Astaire and Rogers at their best. As a dancing partner Kelly is better suited to Hayworth than Astaire.

Cover Girl contains a number of moments which progress the art of presenting dancing on the screen and by far the most significant is Kelly's "Alter Ego" dance, the like of which had never been filmed before—or since. "It was the most difficult thing I've ever done, a technical torture, and I wouldn't want to have to do it again." The setting of the dance is a dim, deserted street late at night, and it springs from the hero's despondency over what he believes to be the loss of his girl. The situation is one of personal conflict, with part of his psyche deeply unhappy and another part trying to tell him it is for the best. To express this Kelly conceived the idea of a double dance, with the two disparate views in visual conflict: Kelly spots his reflection in a shop window and it comes to separate life, jumping into the street to confront him. The two figures pursue each other, leap over each other, run up and down stairs and generally vent their feelings in fancy footwork, all of it of a decidedly tough, masculine nature.

The "Alter Ego" dance came about after the rest of the film had been shot and Harry Cohn, the fabled hard-headed boss of Columbia, told Kelly he would like to see him do a solo. Having outlined his idea, no one at Columbia thought it could be done—but Cohn was convinced and told him to go ahead. Says Kelly: "I wanted to do something that couldn't be done in the theatre. The scene called for a man to show the conflict within himself and on a stage I could have done that easily with a few contortions and a fall to the floor, but I'd found out by now that what worked in a theatre didn't always work on the screen. For example, on the stage I would hoof around for a minute or two and wink at the audience, and they'd love it. But in a film that falls flat—the personality is missing and you have to replace it with something that has meaning for the camera. It's a matter of fitting a three-dimensional art into a two-dimensional medium, and there's nothing easy about it—everything works against you. With this situation I had to invent two dances that could be synchronized, and the main problem was rehearsing the cameraman. We had to use a fixed-head camera in order to get the precision and Stanley Donen—without whom the piece couldn't have been done—would call out the timings for the cameraman, like "one–two–three–stop." We worked for about a month on that dance, then shot it in four days, with a lot more time spent editing all this double-printed footage. Having been told it couldn't be done, I was delighted to bring it off."

Somewhat ironically, Gene Kelly made *Cover Girl* not for MGM, famed for its musicals, but on a loan-out to Columbia. At his own studio he had been unable to persuade his employers to allow him more freedom in devising dances for the screen but with *Cover Girl* in release and bringing him wide acclaim MGM viewed him in a different light. With this picture Kelly's career—and the art of film choreography—took a giant step forward.

The Alter Ego Dance

54

With Rita Hayworth

With Rita Hayworth, director Charles Vidor and Phil Silvers

With Rita Hayworth, Otto Kruger, director Charles Vidor, Eve Arden, Phil Silvers and Leslie Brooks

With Deanna Durbin

CHRISTMAS HOLIDAY

CREDITS:

A Universal Production 1944. Produced by Felix Jackson. Directed by Robert Siodmak. Screenplay by Herman J. Mankiewicz, based on the novel by Somerset Maugham. Photographed by Woody Bredell. Art direction by John B. Goodman and Robert Clatworthy. Edited by Ted Kent. Musical score by Hans J. Salter. Running time: 93 minutes.

CAST:

Jackie Lamont, Abigail Martin: Deanna Durbin; *Robert Manette:* Gene Kelly; *Simon Fenimore:* Richard Whorf; *Charles Mason:* Dean Harens; *Valerie de Merode:* Gladys George; *Mrs. Manette:* Gale Sondergaard; *Gerald Tyler:* David Bruce.

Christmas Holiday is an interesting item. It con-tains Gene Kelly's most offbeat performance, as a charming killer, and it was designed by Universal to give Deanna Durbin her first opportunity with drama. As a teenager she had been the studio's lifesaver, her early musicals having kept Universal from bankruptcy, but with time it became a problem to find suitable vehicles to maintain her popularity as she changed from a girl into a woman. Durbin was twenty-two when she made this picture, and her studio was greatly relieved when it grossed bigger earnings than her previous productions. However, it is neither the performance of Durbin or Kelly that keeps *Christmas Holiday* alive in the minds of film enthusiasts so much as the fact that it is work of the remarkable German director Robert Siodmak. He left Germany in 1934, having offended the Nazis, and settled in Paris, where he continued his career as a filmmaker. Siodmak arrived in Hollywood in

With Richard Whorf and Deanna Durbin

1940, leaving Paris just ahead of the German occupation, and over the course of the next dozen years directed a number of highly regarded films, mostly of the crime-fear-mystery *genre*, the best of them being *The Spiral Staircase* (1945) and *The Killers* (1946).

The screenplay is based, so roughly as to be barely recognizable, on a novel by Somerset Maugham, with the French location of the original switched to Louisiana and the role of the principal character, a girl reduced by dramatic circumstances to prostitution softened to that of a singer-hostess in a second-rate nightclub. The film opens at a military post as a group of officer candidates receive their commissions. One of them, Charles Mason (Dean Harens), is about to leave to visit his fiancee but he receives a telegram from her telling him she has just married someone else. Despondent, he catches a plane to visit his home in San Francisco but because of bad weather the plane is forced down in New Orleans. Mason's depression is increased by his not being able to get a hotel room, and a breezy reporter, Simon Fenimore (Richard Whorf) takes it upon himself to cheer him up. He takes him to the Maison Lafitte and persuades one of the girls, Jackie Lamont (Durbin) to spend some time with him. Jackie herself is quiet and rather glum and the young lieutenant finds himself trying to cheer *her* up. It is Christmas Eve and he offers to take her anywhere she would care to go, and somewhat to his surprise she asks to be taken to church to attend mass.

With Deanna Durbin and the Rev. Neal Dodd, a Hollywood Episcopalian minister frequently used by the studios to perform screen weddings.

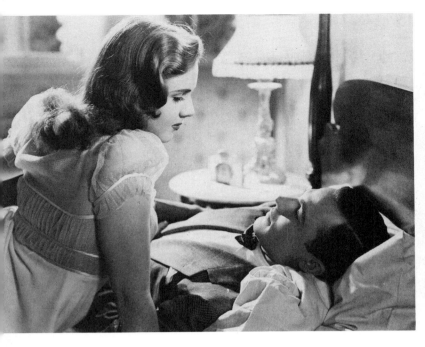

With Deanna Durbin and Gale Sondergaard

With Deanna Durbin

The Christmas mass acts as a catharsis for the unhappy Jackie and with some persuasion she breaks down and tells Mason her story. Her real name is Abigail Martin and she is the wife of a jailed murderer, Robert Manette (Kelly). She had met this charming young man at a symphony concert and after a brief courtship married him and gone to live at the home of his mother (Gale Sondergaard). The Manettes appear to be wealthy and Robert has no occupation, but time proves him to be a psychopath, gambling away the family fortune and getting into trouble. He is always able to charm his wife and smile away their problems, until the day she finds he has unsuccessfully tried to burn a pair of bloodstained trousers. It is soon revealed that Manette has murdered a bookmaker and that his mother has helped him hide the body. Manette is apprehended, convicted and jailed, with the shocked young wife left to fend for herself.

At the end of the film Manette, having escaped prison, appears at the Maison Lafitte in a vengeful mood and threatens his wife with a gun, believing she has betrayed him. Seeing her with the lieutenant increases his resolve to kill her, but before he can do so the police arrive and he is mortally wounded in the subsequent shooting. He dies in her arms, asking to be forgiven, and the audience is left to assume the long-suffering girl will have better luck with the young officer.

Gene Kelly is convincing as the personable cad, as is the remarkable Gale Sondergaard as the fiercely protective mother and her subtle playing suggests a love beyond the norm. The mother-son relationship is one of the best realized aspects of the film, doubtlessly due to Siodmak's direction. In this, as in most of his films, there is a subdued atmosphere of menace, with hints of things unspoken. The style is thoroughly Germanic—slightly cynical and photographed with accent on lighting, on shadows and rays. Unfortunately the film has more style than its substance warrants, but Siodmak was luckier with his next picture, *The Sus-*

pect, starring Charles Laughton, based on the ghastly Crippen murders.

Deanna Durbin was not able to persuade the studio to let her avoid singing in *Christmas Holiday*; in this she sings "Spring Will Be a Little Late This Year," and "Always." Frank Loesser wrote the former especially for the picture and the Irving Berlin song was used as the heroine's pledge to her husband. Miss Durbin, who ended her film career in 1947 and left Hollywood, considers this her best performance, but Gene Kelly recalls her as being nervous and doubtful about it at the time, worrying that the public would not accept this dramatic change in her established image as a lilting, lighthearted singer. For Kelly the film was another loan-out assignment, and one which required no great effort on his part. The commitment was made prior to the release of *Cover Girl*, but with the impact of that picture on the public and the critics, MGM never again loaned Kelly's services to another studio.

With Deanna Durbin

With Frank Sinatra

ANCHORS AWEIGH

CREDITS:

An MGM Production 1945. Produced by Joe Pasternak. Directed by George Sidney. Screenplay by Isobel Lennart, based on a story by Natalie Marcin. Photographed in Technicolor by Robert Planck and Charles Boyle. Art direction by Cedric Gibbons and Randall Duell. Edited by Adrienne Fazan. Musical direction by George Stoll. Songs by Jule Styne (music) and Sammy Cahn (lyrics). Cartoon sequence directed by Fred Quimby. Running time: 143 minutes.

CAST:

Clarence Doolittle: Frank Sinatra; *Susan Abbott:* Kathryn Grayson; *Joseph Brady*; Gene Kelly; *Jose Iturbi:* Himself; *Donald Martin:* Dean Stockwell; *Brooklyn Girl:* Pamela Britton; *Police Sergeant:* Rags Ragland; *Cafe Manager:* Billy Gilbert; *Admiral Hammond:* Henry O'Neill; *Carlos:* Carlos Ramirez; *Police Captain:* Edgar Kennedy; *Bertram Kraler:* Grady Sutton; *Admiral's Aide:* Leon Ames; *Little Beggar Girl:* Sharon McManus.

It was with *Anchors Aweigh* that Gene Kelly came into his own right; the vitality and the joyousness of his performance in this highly entertaining film fairly shouts with the triumph of a man who has hit his own unique stride, and to the approval of every onlooker. This is a kingpin of a musical, filling more than two hours with a variety of music and humor, some of which is now dated due to its wartime slant. But the film retains much of its appeal; its producer, Joe Pasternak, was a man with the Midas touch in popular entertainment and a shrewd judge of talent. He

60

With Sharon McManus

With Kathryn Grayson, Frank Sinatra and Dean Stockwell

allowed Kelly free rein in devising his dance routines, with the happiest of results. *Anchors Aweigh* contains several memorable dances and with his animated sequence, "The King Who Couldn't Dance," Kelly came up with a classic. Pasternak also had the inspired idea of teaming Kelly with Frank Sinatra, who had appeared in five previous movies but never to advantage, despite his being the crooning rage of the day. But as a gawky, girl-shy sailor, Sinatra greatly widened his following with this picture.

The plotline of *Anchors Aweigh* is no more substantial than that of most other movie musicals but it serves as a good thread: two sailors, Joseph Brady and Clarence Doolittle (Kelly and Sinatra) decide to spend their shore leave in Hollywood and take advantage of the hospitality the movie colony is offering servicemen. Joseph, a nautical Don Juan, imagines he will have a field day with the many attractive girls who work in the studios, and that he will also be able to arrange something for his bashful buddy. They meet Susan Abbott (Kathryn Grayson), who works as an extra in the movies while studying to be a singer. She lives with her small brother Donald (Dean Stockwell) and proves to be too conservative for the tastes of Joseph, so he tries to foist her off on Clarence. She does not take kindly to this since she feels a strong attraction to Joseph, and his scheming backfires as he finds himself falling in love with her.

61

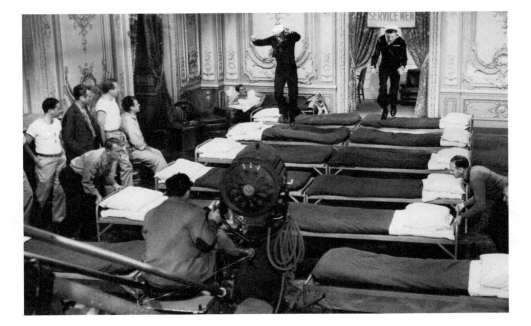

With Frank Sinatra, Kathryn Grayson and Billy Gilbert

Clarence meets a girl from Brooklyn (Pamela Britton) in the Hollywood Canteen and they fall in love. By the end of the picture the two sailors return to their ships having gained the affections of girls likely to be their future wives.

The device of having Kathryn Grayson play a movie extra is the hook on which much of the entertainment hangs. Joseph—and the audience—thereby gain entrance to MGM, and with the girl also a music student auditioning for pianist-conductor Jose Iturbi we get to hear a little popular concert music as well as the songs and dances of Kelly and Sinatra. Iturbi plays a bit of the famous Tchaikowsky concerto and, to prove he's no square, a boogie-woogie version of "The Donkey Serenade." He also accompanies Grayson as she sings "Jalousie." She also sings "All of a Sudden My Heart Sings." Sinatra was well served by the songs written by Jule Styne and Sammy Cahn. He and Kelly sing "We Hate to Leave," a cheeky song of farewell as the holiday-bound gobs leave their comrades, and Sinatra sings a song of fake conquest, "I Begged Her," which is resolved into a sprightly dance for Sinatra and Kelly in a service dormitory. The dance ends with their leaping from bed to bed—actually a series of small trampolines. Sinatra's most charming song is "I Fall in Love Too Easily," and his most maudlin his crooning of Brahms' "Lullaby" to little Dean Stockwell.

Gene Kelly has three major dance routines in *Anchors Aweigh*, in a wide range of style. He does "The Mexican Hat Dance" with a little Mexican girl (Sharon McManus), a very appealing routine somewhat limited by the fact that the partner is a child. But there are no limitations on his elaborate Spanish fandango, using a huge set in the form of a castle and danced like a combination of Rudolph Valentino and Douglas Fairbanks, Sr. The number comes about when Kelly, as the sailor being shown around the film studio by his girlfriend, imagines what it would be like if he were courting her in a costume movie. He dances around a courtyard, scales the walls of the castle, leaps from one parapet to another to reach the balcony of his princess, and leaves by making a huge swing on a hanging drapery from one building to another. And all this to the tune of "La Cumparsita!"

The highlight of *Anchors Aweigh*, and one of the most marvelous pieces of dance-fantasy ever done in films, is the sequence combining a cartoon with live action, "The King Who Couldn't Dance," the basis of which is "The Worry Song," with lyrics by Ralph Freed and music by Sammy

With Jose Iturbi, Frank Sinatra and Pamela Britton

With Henry O'Neill and Frank Sinatra

Fain. The setting is a mythical kingdom, with MGM's familiar Jerry the Mouse as the monarch. William Hanna and Joseph Barbera of the cartoon department and Irving G. Reis of the optical effects department were responsible for the production. The four minutes of screen time involved some ten thousand painted frames to synchronize with Kelly's movements. After devising a meticulous storyboard, Kelly was first photographed doing his part of the sequence, and then the mouse was animated frame by frame. The two figures were later linked optically. The story has Kelly as a French sailor who finds himself in a sad country where dancing is forbidden. He then visits the throne room of the castle and persuades the king to change his mind.

With Jerry, the King Mouse

With Tom and Jerry

The cartoon sequence took two months to complete. It came about through Kelly's desire to do something that had not been done before on film: "Stanley Donen and I sat around for a couple of days trying to think of something and after one long period of silence Stanley suggested, 'How about doing a dance with a cartoon?' This was it. The MGM brass didn't think it could be done, but Pasternak went to bat for us and got a budget of $100,000, to do it as an independent production, warning us that it likely would not appear in the movie. Stanley and I went to Walt Disney, to get his advice and possibly hire some of his men to work for us. But this wasn't possible because the Disney studio was so busy it couldn't accept any extra work. Disney was himself experimenting with live action and animation at that time although he had nothing as difficult in mind as what we hoped to do. But he gave us his blessings, and the fact that Disney considered the idea feasible helped us persuade the MGM cartoon department to do the job. I get all the credit for this, but it would have been impossible for me without Stanley, he worked with the cameraman and called the shots in all these intricate timings and movements. It wasn't easy for the cameraman—he was being asked to photograph something that wasn't there."

Anchors Aweigh was a solid hit wherever it played and it firmly registered Kelly as a star entertainer from whom the public now had the right to expect interesting future performances. It also won him a nomination for the Academy Award.

With Fred Astaire

ZIEGFELD FOLLIES

CREDITS:

An MGM Production 1946. Produced by Arthur Freed. Directed by Vincente Minnelli. Photographed in Technicolor by George Folsey and Charles Rosher. Art direction by Cedric Gibbons, Merrill Pye and Jack Martin Smith. Edited by Albert Akst. Musical direction by Lennie Hayton. Dance direction by Robert Alton. Running time: 118 minutes.

CAST:

Fred Astaire, Lucille Ball, Lucille Bremer, Fanny Brice, Judy Garland, Kathryn Grayson, Lena Horne, Gene Kelly, James Melton, Victor Moore, Red Skelton, Esther Williams, William Powell, Edward Arnold, Marion Bell, Cyd Charisse, Hume Cronyn, William Frawley, Robert Lewis, Virginia O'Brien, and Keenan Wynn.

When *Ziegfeld Follies* was reviewed by the press in New York in March of 1946, several critics made the point that it was a filmed version of the kind of plush, all-star stage revue which was even then a thing of the past. A similar comment can now be made about the film itself. We are never again likely to see such a movie production because the studio system which produced it no longer exists. Gone are the rosters of contracted performers, the stables of producers, directors and writers, and the various departments supplying all the resources the creators could possibly want. *Ziegfeld Follies* is, perhaps, the greatest of all Hollywood musicals although it is difficult to compare it to others because it has no plot at all; it is a collection of twelve unrelated segments of music and

With Fred Astaire

With Fred Astaire

With Fred Astaire

comedy using as its connective tissue the premise that if Florenz Ziegfeld had been able to return from the grave, this is the show he would have produced—assuming that he had MGM at his command.

William Powell appears at the start of the film in the guise of Ziegfeld (Powell had played the fabulous showman in the 1936 picture *The Great Ziegfeld*), occupying a plush apartment in Heaven. He muses about a new show and draws up a list of possible stars. After a puppet sequence—depicting some of Ziegfeld's early stars—Fred Astaire addresses the audience and pays tribute to Ziegfeld, thereby touching off the fantasy revue. The real producer of the show, Arthur Freed, is, of course, never seen—but it might be said that he out-Ziegfelded his subject.

The twelve sections, averaging eight to ten minutes each, are:

1. "Bring on the Beautiful Girls," a girlie merry-go-round with Lucille Ball as the ring mistress, and Virginia O'Brien singing a satirical ditty in praise of men—a counterpoint to the usual Ziegfeldian stand.
2. "A Water Ballet" starring Esther Williams and her aquabatics in an exotic marine setting.
3. "The Drinking Song," from Verdi's *La Traviata*, sung by James Melton and Marion Bell.
4. "Pay the Two Dollars," a classic sketch with Victor Moore as a man fined for spitting in a subway and Edward Arnold as the lawyer who refuses to allow him to pay the fine, making an issue of the case and causing Moore to be jailed.
5. "This Heart of Mine," a dance story with Fred Astaire and Lucille Bremer.
6. "Number Please," a skit with Keenan Wynn ribbing the telephone operator's errors in giving wrong numbers.
7. "Love," a sensuous torch song by Lena Horne.
8. "When Television Comes," with Red Skelton imagining the future problems of commercial announcers on TV, in particular those dispensing liquor.
9. "Limehouse Blues," a dramatic ballet with Fred Astaire and Lucille Bremer.
10. "The Great Lady Has an Interview," with Judy Garland lampooning a celebrated actress about to portray a lady inventor.
11. "The Babbit and the Bromide," a comedy dance by Fred Astaire and Gene Kelly.
12. "There's Beauty Everywhere," with Kathryn Grayson singing in a fantastic setting of multi-

colored bubbles and surrealistic shapes, that looks like a blend of Dali and Busby Berkeley, but isn't.

Ziegfeld Follies has much to recommend it and one of its better numbers is "The Babbitt and the Bromide," marking the only appearance together in a film by Fred Astaire and Gene Kelly. The decision to use this piece of material was made by Arthur Freed, who had seen Fred and his sister Adele do the number in the 1927 Broadway musical *Funny Face*, for which George and Ira Gershwin provided the songs. Freed also considered it a good idea to use the two dancers together, since Kelly by this time had been hailed as a rival to Astaire's position as the premier Hollywood dancer, with some assumption by the public that there might be jealousy between them. Says Freed: "There was no rivalry at all, each is a genuine admirer of the other. My only problem was their deference for each other. Each was willing to do whichever dance the other wanted. I had suggested Babbitt-Bromide to Fred and he liked the idea, but after the first rehearsal Gene privately told me he didn't think too much of the material. I mentioned this to Fred, who then said we should drop it and do whatever Gene wanted, which was an Indian dance and song written for him by Ralph Blane and Hugh Martin. But when Gene heard this he said no, we should do the number that Fred liked. It was a real Alphonse and Gaston routine."

"The Babbitt and the Bromide," is, truth to tell, not a great piece of material and it is a pity that in their only work together they could not have agreed on something more substantial. The routine concerns a pair of gentleman acquaintances, both glib bores, who meet at intervals in their lives and cheerily mouth the same clichéd greetings, "Hello, how are you? Howzafolks? What's new?" and a whole stream of vacuous comments, none of which ever registers in the mind of the other. Part of the lyrics give the narrative of the plot, the fact that they are young men when they first meet and angels in Heaven at the end—but always saying the same things. Their characters are limned in fancy, identical footwork by Astaire and Kelly, all of it bright and bouncing, and giving the viewer an opportunity to compare the two dancers. However, little comparison can be made because the routine is typical of neither one, except to state the obvious facts that Astaire is a lighter man and a shade more graceful, and that Kelly is more muscular and a little more forceful because of it.

Astaire and Kelly rehearsed the dance for a week and shot it in two days during May of 1944, but it was a full two years before *Ziegfeld Follies* was ready for showing, by which time Gene Kelly had been in and out of the United States Navy.

With Fred Astaire

Rehearsing with Astaire

LIVING IN A BIG WAY

CREDITS:

An MGM Production 1947. Produced by Pandro S. Berman. Directed by Gregory LaCava. Screenplay by Gregory La Cava and Irving Ravetch. Photographed by Harold Rosson. Art direction by Cedric Gibbons and Williams Ferrari. Edited by Ferris Webster. Musical score by Lennie Hayton. Running time: 103 minutes.

CAST:

Leo Gogarty: Gene Kelly; *Margaud Morgan:* Marie McDonald; *D. Rutherford Morgan:* Charles Winninger; *Peggy Randall:* Phyllis Thaxter; *Mrs. Morgan:* Spring Byington; *Abigail Morgan:* Jean Adair; *Everett Hanover Smythe:* Clinton Sundberg; *Stuart:* John Warburton; *Schultz:* William "Bill" Phillips; *Attorney Ambridge:* John Alexander; *Annie Pearl:* Phyllis Kennedy; *Dolly:* Bernadine Hayes.

When Gene Kelly concluded his naval service in early 1946 he advised MGM of his availability and found they had nothing immediately prepared for him. The studio at that time had the problem of finding vehicles for a number of stars returning to the fold after years away in the services, and Kelly's experience in this regard proved to be typical. Not having danced for two years he moved to get himself back into form by practicing at a studio in New York, and it was while limbering up that he received a phone call from an excited Louis B. Mayer, telling him he had just signed to a contract Marie McDonald, a beautiful blonde they would publicize as "The Body" and that he wanted Kelly to co-star with her in a film to be written and directed by Gregory La Cava. Since La Cava had a good reputation, as a kind

With Marie McDonald

turned over as living quarters for returning servicemen. Mr. Morgan has grown wealthy during the war—a hint of profiteering—and his daughter has become spoiled and pampered in the process. He therefore looks upon the level-headed Leo as a sensible addition to the family, a sentiment felt even more strongly by Margaud's feisty old grandmother Abigail (Jean Adair), who backs Leo in his plans for building a housing project for veterans. Margaud gradually changes her mind about Leo—and he about her. They both blow hot and cold in their feelings and finally agree on a divorce, but at the hearing the judge decides against a decree to end the marriage, to the relief of both Leo and Margaud.

Without its interpolated musical moments *Living in a Big Way* would barely qualify as a Grade B supporting feature, and without Kelly it would have almost no vitality. The performances of Charles Winninger and Spring Byington as the scatterbrained parents are charming and Phyllis Thaxter is pleasing as a war widow who secretly loves Kelly because he reminds her of her husband.

All that can be said for Marie McDonald in this film is that she is pretty of face and figure. Mayer's faith in her future was completely misfounded;

of minor-league Ernst Lubitsch, Kelly agreed. Upon meeting La Cava he found there was no script, only a hazy outline—Irving Ravetch was hired to work on the screenplay with La Cava—and after working with Marie McDonald for a few days it was apparent the girl had very little ability as an actress. When *Living in a Big Way* (a senseless title) was completed, MGM then asked Kelly to invent several musical sequences to add to it, to make the shallow picture marketable. The effort proved to be in vain.

The story: Army lieutenant Leo Gogarty (Kelly) woos and marries the lovely Margaud Morgan (Marie McDonald) after only a few days of courtship, and gets orders to proceed overseas immediately, barely an hour or so after the wedding. He returns three years later, eagerly looking forward to his delayed honeymoon but instead receiving the cold shoulder from Margaud, who informs him that all hasty wartime marriages are a mistake and that she wants a divorce. Gogarty disagrees, so do her parents (Charles Winninger and Spring Byington) who take a liking to Leo and offer him accommodation in an old house of theirs they have

With Phyllis Thaxter and Jimmy Hunt

With Marie McDonald

72

she never won respect as an actress and seemingly suffered a similar lack of luck in her private life. She died in 1965 at the age of forty-two. *Living in a Big Way* was a sad letdown for Gregory La Cava; it proved to be his last film, and he died two years later. La Cava had been a cartoonist before making films, and in Hollywood he was appreciated for his humor and his direction of several stylish comedies, among them *My Man Godfrey* (1936) and *Stage Door* (1937).

In the original script *Living in a Big Way* called for Kelly to do a dance with Marie McDonald to the tune of "It Had to Be You," but three routines, of Kelly's invention, were added later. One is a dance with an amazingly well-trained dog, "Fido and Me," another is Kelly's comedic dance-serenade to a large female statue, and the most elaborate one takes place on a building project with a group of children. The dance is built around children's games, and later involves Kelly performing all over a half-completed apartment house. He feels, somewhat ruefully, that his dance creations for this film are among his best but he takes some consolation in this largely lost work in that it brought him praise from the esteemed American dancer-choreographer, Martha Graham.

With Judy Garland

THE PIRATE

CREDITS:

An MGM Production 1948. Produced by Arthur Freed. Directed by Vincente Minnelli. Screenplay by Albert Hackett and Frances Goodrich based on the play by S. N. Behrman. Songs by Cole Porter. Musical direction by Lennie Hayton. Photographed in Technicolor by Harry Stradling. Art direction by Cedric Gibbons and Jack Martin Smith. Edited by Blanche Sewell. Running time: 101 minutes.

CAST:

Manuela: Judy Garland; *Serafin:* Gene Kelly; *Don Pedro Vargas:* Walter Slezak; *Aunt Inez:* Gladys Cooper; *The Advocate:* Reginald Owen; *The Viceroy:* George Zucco; *Gandsmith Brothers:* Nicholas Brothers; *Uncle Capucho:* Lester Allen; *Isabella:* Lola Deem; *Mercedes:* Ellen Ross; *Lizarda:* Mary Jo Ellis; *Casilda:* Jean Dean; *Eloise:* Marion Murray; *Gumbo:* Ben Lessy; *Bolo:* Jerry Bergen; *Juggler:* Val Setz; *Trillo:* Cully Richards.

Vincente Minnelli, the son of an Italian violinist and a French actress, grew up in a theatre environment and showed a talent for artistic design while still a boy. At sixteen he was employed by Balaban and Katz as a designer of costumes and scenery and by the time he was twenty-three he was the art director of Radio City Music Hall in New York. This eventually led to Minnelli's becoming a director of stage musicals, and in 1940 he was brought to Hollywood by Arthur Freed. He put in two years as a handyman-designer-advisor-director of musical sequences in Freed productions, and was finally assigned as director of *Cabin in the Sky*. With his directing of the exceptional *Meet Me in St. Louis*, it was clear to all that Minnelli was a director of unusual artistry and sensitivity, and the only man Arthur Freed would consider using as director of *The Pirate*. Freed had purchased the rights to the stage play especially for Judy Garland, who was by now Mrs. Minnelli, and Gene Kelly jumped at the opportunity to play the male lead since it offered not only the chance to sing and dance in a bravura period setting, but also to indulge in some swashbuckling, for which he had a definite taste.

The Pirate was made in an atmosphere of loving care and enthusiasm. Freed contracted Cole Porter to write the song-score and after he had written it, with the film well into production Gene Kelly visited Porter and implored him to write an additional song, a knock-about clown number for Judy and himself. And as soon as Freed heard "Be a Clown," it was written into the script. The screenplay is based on the stage comedy S. N. Behrman wrote for Alfred Lunt and Lynn Fontanne, and produced by the Theatre Guild in 1943, which in turn was based on a 1911 German play, *Der Seeräuber* by Ludwig Fulda. In the original the main character was a notorious pirate who retires and, under a new name, becomes the respectable mayor of a little town in the Caribbean. In his version Behrman made this a secondary theme, giving the leading strains to a young, romantic girl who dreams of a legendary pirate and an itinerant actor who impersonates the pirate in order to win her love. The humor rises from the actual pirate, now an older man, not only being the mayor of the town but being engaged to the girl and unable to reveal his identity. This is also the thematic material of the film. Minnelli saw this as the basis for a fantasy-parody of operetta form, and the end result is a sumptuous, highly imaginative and sophisticated movie musical. He and Kelly were completely in accord in this approach, with Kelly deliberately setting out to caricature his part in the style of the elder Fairbanks and John Barrymore in his last, flamboyantly hammy years.

As if to warn the audience of its fairy-tale intent, *The Pirate* opens with a dainty hand turning the pages of a book about Black Macoco, a feared pirate of the Spanish Main, and an enthralled girlish voice reading his exploits. The hand and the voice belong to Manuela (Garland), the daughter of a wealthy house. Her dreams are shattered by her Aunt Inez (Gladys Cooper), who informs

During a break with Judy Garland

With Judy Garland

Manuela that a good marriage has been arranged for her with Don Pedro Vargas (Walter Slezak), the affluent mayor of their town, San Sebastian. Don Pedro is a rotund, bumbling social climber, and the idea of marriage with him does not please Manuela. On a shopping trip into the town to purchase things for her wedding she notices Serafin (Kelly) and his troupe of entertainers, who have just arrived and who make their presence known to the townspeople. As his troupe prepare for their evening performance, the amorous Serafin wanders around the town eyeing the girls and calling each one of them Niña. A puzzled merchant asks him why and Serafin launches into a song and dance by way of explanation—Niña is his generic name for all beautiful women. He glides from one lovely girl to the next, beaming at each and serenading with lines like: "Niña, you're so sweet, I mean ya, fairly drive me wild!" and "I'll be having neurasthenia, 'til I make you mine." Serafin scales walls and leaps from balcony to balcony, across a roof and down a drainpipe into the street, all the time passing from girl to girl and after dancing in the town square he artfully winds up next to a poster advertising his show.

The only Niña Serafin fails to amuse is Manuela, who finds him annoying and hammy. But that night, unable to sleep, she wanders into town to see his show. Serafin is about to dazzle his audience with an act of mesmerism and needing a subject he chooses Manuela. He hypnotizes her and in a trance she confesses she has a dream lover, a handsome pirate who will one day sweep down and carry her away. So intense is her passion that she breaks into song and extols this paragon, "Mack the Black." The audience applaud her and Serafin brings her back from the trance with a kiss. Indignantly she takes her leave. Later, while trying on her wedding gown in her bedroom, she looks out the window to find that Serafin has followed her. He has also strung a tightrope leading to her window and as he makes his way across the wire to her, she cautions him, "No, it looks so bad," but the ardent lover persists and enters the room to theatrically plead his case. Don Pedro arrives, whip in hand, but before he can flog Serafin, the actor takes him aside and tells the mayor he recognizes him—he is Macoco, whom Serafin once encountered on the high seas. Don Pedro begs him to keep it secret, thinking that his identity as a former pirate would spoil his marriage. He is unaware of Manuela's enchant-

With Walter Slezak

wounded performer to defend his art, "I have a review . . . comparing me with David Garrick . . ." But Manuela explodes in fury and pelts him with every object she can lay her hands to, leaving the room covered with broken china and bric-a-brac. As the poor actor lies unconscious on the floor, Manuela realizes her true feelings for him and, with his head cradled on her lap, she sings "You Can Do No Wrong." Their idyll is interupted by Don Pedro, arriving with a company of militia and arresting Serafin as a jewel thief—having already planted the evidence in the actor's trunk.

Sentenced to hang, Serafin asks for a last request, a farewell performance, and over Don Pedro's objections the Viceroy (George Zucco) gives his approval. Serafin has decided to depart the world with a happy song and dance, "Be a Clown," which he does with a pair of equally athletic black dancers (The Nicholas Brothers). Meanwhile, Manuela notices that her engagement ring matches the jewelry planted in Serafin's trunk, and guesses the real culprit. After his dance Serafin tries to mesmerize Don Pedro, but Aunt Inez interrupts. Sensing what he is trying to do, Manuela fakes a trance

ment with the name of Macoco. But Serafin spots his opportunity and rushes into the street to proclaim himself the famed pirate. Soldiers attack him but he easily wards them off as the astounded Manuela looks from her window. The romantic girl fantasizes and imagines herself joining him in his exploits. In this, "The Pirate Ballet," Serafin, in boldly heroic guise, leads his ferocious men, fights off enemies, swings through the rigging of his ship, taunts danger in a fire dance and celebrates his capture of booty with a fearful spear dance. The sequence is an exhaustingly acrobatic, lurid abstract.

Serafin announces he will raze the town unless Manuela is brought to him. He takes possession of the mayor's house, knowing Don Pedro can't object, and the townspeople beg Manuela to sacrifice herself. She feigns terror, as she eagerly prepares herself for the rendezvous. But once in the mayor's house she overhears a servant who accidentally reveals that Serafin is pretending to be the pirate. Before he can confess the ruse Manuela tells him she knew all the time that he was an actor, and not a very good one, which leads the

78

With Judy Garland

and he leads her onto the stage where she denounces Don Pedro as a miserable, miserly coward, a man who is "even afraid to go to sea." She states her undying devotion to the memory of Macoco and sings "Love of My Life," ending the passionate song with a kiss for Serafin. Don Pedro can stand it no longer, he leaps on the stage and yells at Manuela, "If you want to worship Macoco, worship *me!*" He pulls out a pistol to kill Serafin but other members of the troupe attack and disarm him. Serafin then announces the new star of his show, Manuela, and together in clown costumes and makeup they sing a spirited reprise of "Be a Clown."

In the opinion of many film enthusiasts, *The Pirate* is among the most marvelous of all Hollywood musicals. The script is witty and highly literate, although possibly a bit too "inside" in its show-business allusions. The sets and costumes are delightful, the color photography of Harry Stradling is the work of a master, the songs are top-notch Porter, the direction of Vincente Minnelli is an almost perfect balance of story and music, and the performances of Garland and Kelly reflect their obvious love of working together. Despite all this, *The Pirate* came close to being a flop in the first year of its release. The critics hailed it but the mass movie audience resisted it. Many of the top MGM executives disliked it, feeling it was too different and too artistic for the fans, and Louis B. Mayer ordered "The Pirate Ballet" changed and reshot—in his view the original was far too erotic. One number, "Voodoo," was eliminated. Ludicrous as this managerial stand may seem on the aesthetic level, it certainly was borne out by the reaction of the public, who obviously wanted the simple, appealing Garland and not a sophisticated comedienne. Similarly it proved to Gene Kelly that it was dangerous to step far from his image as the likable, all-American hoofer. Some years later Arthur Freed made the comment that *The Pirate* was twenty years ahead of its time, and

"Be a Clown!" with Judy Garland

the reception the film now receives when shown to film students proves him right.

It was a disappointment for Gene Kelly: "I had decided on this Fairbanks-Barrymore approach to the role at the very start and Minnelli entirely agreed with it. It didn't occur to us until the picture hit the public that what we had done was indulge in a huge inside joke. The sophisticates probably grasped it—all three of them—but the film died in the hinterlands. It was done tongue-in-cheek but it didn't come off, and that's my fault. But I thought Judy was superb—what Minnelli did with color and design in that film is as fine as anything that has ever been done."

The Kelly performance may have puzzled the fans, but his singing and dancing in *The Pirate* are among his best work in films. "Niña" is almost perfect as a saucy Don Juan testament—the number has such fluidity and is so expertly edited that it gives the illusion of being shot in a single take, and musically it is Cole Porter's neat little

With director Vincente Minnelli

With the Nicholas Bros.

satire on Ravel's *Bolero*. "The Pirate Ballet" is an astonishing piece of business in its athletics, although the original concept of it as a love dance —a manifestation of Manuela's romanticism— would have made more sense. "Be a Clown" is a classic statement of its kind and Kelly's dancing with the memorable Nicholas Brothers is thoroughly zesty. Kelly chose the brothers to work with him in this routine, despite the warning of MGM that the sight of a white man dancing with blacks would cost them a few bookings in southern states, which turned out to be the case. As soon as the studio detected lack of success with *The Pirate,* they immediately assigned Garland and Kelly to *Easter Parade,* a more conventional musical vehicle aimed directly at the tastes of the fans and planned to recoup any possible loss of interest in the stars. But Kelly broke his ankle during rehearsals and suggested to Louis B. Mayer that Fred Astaire be contacted as a replacement. Astaire had been retired for two years but he had been showing signs of wanting to get back to work. Says Kelly, "I was pleased to be responsible for getting Fred back but every time I see him and Judy singing 'A Couple of Swells' I do get a twinge of regret."

With Van Heflin, Gig Young
and Robert Coote

THE THREE MUSKETEERS

CREDITS:

An MGM Production 1948. Produced by Pandro S. Berman. Directed by George Sidney. Screenplay by Robert Ardrey, based on the novel by Alexandre Dumas. Photographed in Technicolor by Robert Planck. Art direction by Cedric Gibbons and Malcolm Brown. Edited by Robert J. Kern and George Boemler. Musical score by Herbert Stothart, based on themes by Tchaikowsky. Running time: 126 minutes.

CAST:

Lady de Winter: Lana Turner; *D'Artagnan:* Gene Kelly; *Constance:* June Allyson; *Athos:* Van Heflin; *Queen Anne:* Angela Lansbury; *King Louis XIII:* Frank Morgan; *Richelieu:* Vincent Price; *Planchet:* Keenan Wynn; *The Duke of Bucking-* *ham:* John Sutton; *Porthos:* Gig Young; *Aramis:* Robert Coote; *Treville:* Reginald Owen; *Rochefort:* Ian Keith; *Kitty:* Patricia Medina; *Albert:* Richard Stapley.

Alexandre Dumas's splendid, swashbuckling adventure story of a young cavalier named D'Artagnan and his friendship with three of King Louis XIII's musketeers has been a favorite subject of the movies almost from the beginning of the medium. Aside from numerous European versions, there were several American attempts even before the famous filming by Douglas Fairbanks, Sr. in 1921. Walter Abel was a not very inspiring D'Artagnan at RKO in 1935 and Don Ameche and the Ritz Brothers did a musical lampoon at Fox in 1939. By far the most ambitious attempt to put *The Three Musketeers* on the screen was

With Ian Keith

With Sol Gorss

MGM's 1948 production, on which they lavished two-and-a-half million dollars—then a considerable budget. Gene Kelly was a natural choice for D'Artagnań; he was in the peak of athletic condition and looking a dozen years younger than his actual age of thirty-six. Says Kelly, "I loved playing this part. As a boy I idolized Fairbanks, Sr. and I raised myself to be a gymnast."

Robert Ardrey's screenplay hews fairly closely to the original, necessarily capsulizing it somewhat but giving it a more comedic slant than Dumas intended. This is a weakness in the film and its general tongue-in-cheek tone diminishes the overall effectiveness of the handsome production values and the visual splendor. Nevertheless, this is a version hard to resist as pure entertainment. Its familiar beginning has the young D'Artagnan leaving his country home and proceeding to Paris with a letter of introduction to the commander of the musketeers, Treville (Reginald Owen) but *en passant* he is humiliated by an arrogant nobleman, Rochefort (Ian Keith), who cannot be bothered to duel with the young man and has one of his henchmen knock him out. In Paris D'Artagnan enrolls in the King's service as a musketeer but from Treville's office he spots Rochefort in the street. In a mad dash to catch him D'Artagnan bumps into veteran musketeer Athos (Van Heflin) then Porthos (Gig Young), and then Aramis (Robert Coote), accepting challenges from each one— at the same time and place, in the gardens behind the Luxembourg. D'Artagnan loses Rochefort but he keeps the appointment with the musketeers, offering to fight all three together if they wish. Athos, as the senior challenger, has priority and soon finds the youngster is a brilliant swordsman. A party of guards in the employ of Cardinal Richelieu (Vincent Price) arrive to arrest the musketeers for breaking the Cardinal's rule outlawing dueling, but D'Artagnan joins with the musketeers and together they thoroughly trounce the guards.

The musketeers have immediate cause to serve King Louis XIII (Frank Morgan). Richelieu is plotting to overthrow the King by promoting war with England. It has come to the attention of Richelieu that Queen Anne (Angela Lansbury) is having an affair with the Duke of Buckingham (John Sutton) and he commands his mistress, the beautiful Lady de Winter (Lana Turner) to conspire in an attempt to discredit the Queen. The Queen's lady-in-waiting, Constance (June Allyson) overhears information concerning the gift of the

Queen's necklace to Buckingham, which information Richelieu will use to his advantage. Constance tells this to D'Artagnan, with whom she has fallen in love, and this pains the young man because he has fallen in love with Lady de Winter. It becomes the mission of the musketeers to ride to Calais, cross the Channel to England, retrieve the necklace from Buckingham and return it to the Queen in time for her to wear at an official function, thereby foiling Richelieu's plan to discredit her in public for not having the necklace in her possession. This retrieval has to take place in short order, and D'Artagnan and the musketeers are hounded all the way by Richelieu's guards. But with their mission accomplished, the Cardinal is forced to drop his plans and deny any complicity, which denial costs Lady de Winter her life. It also enables D'Artagnan to settle his score with Rochefort, dispatching him forever.

This spanking production of *The Three Muske-* *teers* suffers from some bad casting: the beautiful Lana Turner and June Allyson are less than comfortable in period costumes and situations, Gig Young and Robert Coote make rather limp musketeers and Frank Morgan, his genial comic image against him, is no King. Angela Lansbury is, however, elegant as the Queen and the late Van Heflin powerful as the moody Athos, a tough man capable of crying in his beer at memories of past loves. As the evil Richelieu Vincent Price is urbanity personified. None of the acting, whether good or mediocre, is helped by the musical scoring of Herbert Stothart who made a major error in deciding to use popular themes by Tchaikowsky as his motifs. In the many excellent action sequences of this film the scoring is acceptable but in using the love theme from *Romeo and Juliet* as a surging accompaniment for scenes between D'Artagnan and Constance, the effect is ludicrous. Balanced against this demerit is the gorgeous Technicolor

With Frank Morgan, Reginald Owen, Van Heflin, Gig Young and Robert Coote

With Van Heflin, Gig Young and Robert Coote

With John Sutton and June Allyson

With Lana Turner

photography of Robert Planck and the art direction of Cedric Gibbons and Malcolm Brown. The film is visually magnificent, and George Sidney's direction is excellent in the pacing of the action, although too languid in the dialogue passages.

But *The Three Musketeers* is Gene Kelly's picture, and without his dashing D'Artagnan it would be much the poorer. Some critics found his bouncing, tumbling, vaulting, flipping and leaping performance tending toward burlesque, but it is entirely conceivable that the man Dumas described as the finest swordsman in France would be this kind of zesty athlete. Other critics pointed out that no other actor had ever come this close to matching the performances of Fairbanks, Sr. at his swashbuckling best. In his article "Swordplay on the Screen," for the June–July, 1965, issue of

With Angela Lansbury and June Allyson

With Vincent Price and Ian Keith

Films in Review, Rudy Behlmer dealt at length with Kelly's D'Artagnan:

MGM . . . hired Jean Heremans, a Belgian fencing champion who succeeded Uyttenhove * as fencing instructor at the Los Angeles Athletic Club, to work out fencing routines for Gene Kelly. . . . The resulting action scenes were strikingly set up and executed, and are among the best of their kind. The early encounter of D'Artagnan, Athos, Porthos and Aramis with the Cardinal's Guards—filmed at (the old) Busch Gardens in Pasadena—was particularly effective. As this sequence progresses and the Cardinal's Guards are being disposed of, D'Artagnan singles out Jussac, Captain of the Guard (Saul Gorss), and the two engage in an acrobatic—and comedic—choreographed routine, accompanied by burlesqued Tchaikowsky. It runs five minutes, and was, up to that time, the longest duel on record. It's a delight.

In later, more serious action sequences, Kelly proved he could help set up and perform—straight—far-from-standard acrobatic feats.

Heremans appeared, in various costumes and makeups, as several different fencers throughout this film, and in an extended fight with Kelly on the beach he finally fell backward into the surf following Kelly's death thrust.

Since screen duels are routined in a manner similar to musical numbers, and since Kelly's dancing style emphasizes a strong, vigorous line and athletic movement, he was able to make the transition from musical comedy to swashbuckling heroics with ease.

Of his nonmusical films, *The Three Musketeers* is Gene Kelly's favorite. MGM continues to earn money from this constantly profitable picture, and on his tours for the U.S. State Department Kelly finds himself followed by small boys in distant lands and greeted as D'Artagnan: "I was in Ghana some years ago and arrived in a town where *The Three Musketeers* had only just played. Hundreds of kids with shining black faces happily trooped after me. At the same time the Russians had sent a lady cosmonaut as their goodwill ambassador but when I showed up the kids deserted her *en masse* to cheer D'Artagnan. I'm very happy to have made that picture, although it didn't get me what I was really after, which was to do a musical version of *Cyrano de Bergerac.* I love the part and although I knew I couldn't, because of my American speech, handle the original text I did believe I could manage a musical version. I pestered MGM for years on that one but I could never get them to go for it."

* Henry J. Uyttenhove, Belgian fencing master and the coach of Fairbanks, Sr. on *The Mark of Zorro* (1920), *The Three Musketeers* (1921) and *Robin Hood* (1922).

88

With Van Heflin

With John Sutton

With Van Heflin

With Sol Gorss

With John Heremans

With June Allyson

90

With Vera-Ellen

WORDS AND MUSIC

CREDITS:

An MGM Production 1948. Produced by Arthur Freed. Directed by Norman Taurog. Screenplay by Fred Finklehoffe, based on a story by Guy Bolton and Jean Halloway, adapted by Ben Feiner, Jr. Photographed in Technicolor by Charles Rosher and Harry Stradling. Art direction by Cedric Gibbons and Jack Martin Smith. Edited by Albert Akst and Ferris Webster. Musical direction by Lennie Hayton. Musical numbers staged and directed by Robert Alton. Running time: 119 minutes.

CAST:

Lorenz Hart: Mickey Rooney; *Richard Rodgers:* Tom Drake; *Herbert Fields:* Marshall Thompson; *Dorothy Feiner:* Janet Leigh; *Peggy Lorgan McNeil:* Betty Garrett; *Joyce Harmon:* Ann Sothern; *Eddie Lorrison Anders:* Perry Como; *Mrs. Hart:* Jeanette Nolan; *Shoe Clerk:* Clinton Sundberg; *Dr. Rodgers:* Harry Antrim; *Ben Feiner, Jr.:* Richard Quine; *Mrs. Rodgers:* Ilka Gruning; *Mr. Feiner:* Emory Parnell; *Mrs. Feiner:* Helen Spring; *James Fernby Kelly:* Edward Earle.

Most of the major American songwriters have been saluted in Hollywood biographies, but seldom with any accuracy. Perhaps this is to be expected; these films exist only as showcases, as convenient marshaling grounds for the creations of the subject being honored. The career struggles of composers and lyricists tend to a sameness, and of interest mainly to students of music or the theatre. Be that as it may, MGM could have done a lot better for Richard Rodgers and Lorenz Hart than *Words and Music.* In this vapid account, Richard Rodgers, a tough-minded and shrewd producer as well as gifted composer is played in bland manner by Tom Drake, and Mickey Rooney frenetically struts around as the brilliant but tragic Lorenz Hart. The selection of music is generous, touching on nearly two dozen songs of the celebrated team and in some instances the performances are excellent. Lena Horne sings "The Lady is a Tramp" in a magnificently sultry manner, and "Blue Room" is smoothly sung by Perry Como and equally smoothly danced by Cyd Charisse.

The most prestigious segment of *Words and Music* is "Slaughter on Tenth Avenue," choreographed and danced by Gene Kelly, with Vera-Ellen as his partner. The piece was originally presented on Broadway in 1937 as the finale of the musical comedy *On Your Toes,* for which Rodgers and Hart wrote the book, along with George Abbott, as well as the music and lyrics. By the time "Slaughter on Tenth Avenue" appeared in *Words and Music,* it was long familiar as a pop concert selection, but in 1937 it was applauded as a milestone in the American theatre —the first presentation of modern ballet in a Broadway musical. It was, in fact, choreographed by the esteemed George Balanchine, and danced by a young Ray Bolger, who appeared in *On Your Toes* as the dancing son of vaudevillian parents. In its original setting the material was more comedic than as choreographed by Kelly for the film; it had Bolger dancing himself into exhaustion to elude capture by a group of gangsters. For the film Kelly shortened the ballet from eleven to seven minutes, truncating some of the lyrical passages, playing up the dramatic substance and inventing a new story. In Kelly's version the dancer is a tough guy in a low-life section of New York, who falls for a pretty street girl but loses her when a former boyfriend, a jealous hood, shoots and kills her.

Kelly's "Slaughter" is set in a sleazy neighborhood, alongside New York's elevated railway and in a large saloon peopled by gangsters and prostitutes, loafers and police. The opening notes of the music suggest the feisty atmosphere and the cheeky character of Kelly's Dancer, who is first seen in his bedroom stretching and yawning, and then proceeding in a cocky, gymnastic style to the street, wearing a sweatshirt, a beret and dark, tight pants. He spots a blonde (Vera-Ellen) in a yellow sweater and a green slit skirt, and when she notices his interest she responds with a seductive dance

With Vera-Ellen

92

around a lamp post. The mood of the music turns romantic and it becomes clear the two are smitten with each other. The music changes again to a cheerful, breezy theme as they enter the saloon together and dance happily; the music takes on a more serious tone as the dancers begin to feel more concerned, then bold and jazzy as they realize their feelings are mutual. The joyful dance is interrupted by the appearance of a rival and he and Kelly engage in a mimed fight-dance. Police arrive and quell the fighting. The hubbub subsides and a wailing oboe sets a mood of uneasy peace. After the police leave the violence flairs up and in the ensuing melee the girl is shot and flung down a flight of stairs. Kelly and the rival then break into a savage fight, which ends with Kelly being shot. He slides along the floor to the body of the girl, picks her up and carries her to the top of the stairs, where he collapses and lies dying and embracing the girl, as the music swells to a bittersweet ending.

As it had on Broadway in 1937, "Slaughter on Tenth Avenue" broke new ground when it was seen in *Words and Music* in 1948. It was the first long, complete piece of modern ballet in a Hollywood film and it proved that a wide audience would accept such artistry if presented in a vital, interesting manner. It was another triumph for Gene Kelly in his efforts to bring worthwhile dancing to the screen, and the piece was also an excellent showcase for his muscular, masculine style. The tightly paced seven-minute production took three days to shoot, following almost four weeks of rehearsal. Kelly regards Vera-Ellen as among the very best women dancers in films, and she herself looks upon "Slaughter" as the best work of her Hollywood career. The dance called for characterization, gymnastics and drama, and it received all this in full measure from Kelly and Vera-Ellen.

94

TAKE ME OUT TO THE BALL GAME

CREDITS:

An MGM Production 1949. Produced by Arthur Freed. Directed by Busby Berkeley. Screenplay by Harry Tugend and George Wells. Based on a story by Gene Kelly and Stanley Donen. Photographed in Technicolor by George Folsey. Art direction by Cedric Gibbons and Daniel B. Cathcart. Edited by Blanche Sewell. Songs by Betty Comden, Adolph Green and Roger Edens. Musical direction by Adolph Deutsch. Running time: 94 minutes.

CAST:

Dennis Ryan: Frank Sinatra; *K. C. Higgins:* Esther Williams; *Eddie O'Brien:* Gene Kelly; *Shirley Delwyn:* Betty Garrett; *Joe Lorgan:* Edward Arnold; *Nat Goldberg:* Jules Munshin; *Michael Gilhuly:* Richard Lane; *Slappy Burke:* Tom Dugan; *Zalinka:* Murray Alper; *Nick Donford:* William Graff; *Henchmen:* Mack Gray and Charles Regan; *Steve:* Saul Gorss; *Karl:* Douglas Fowley; *Dr. Winston:* Eddie Parkes; *Cop in Park:* James Burke.

The idea behind *Take Me Out to the Ball Game* sprang from the fact that there was once a pair of American vaudevillians, around the turn of the century, who were baseball fanatics and spent their summers playing with professional leagues. Gene Kelly and Stanley Donen developed this into a simple plot outline and took it to Arthur Freed. He liked it and assigned Harry Tugend and George Wells to flesh it out into a comedy-musical, with lyrics by Betty Comden and Adolph Green, and music by Roger Edens.

Kelly and Donen asked Freed if they could direct the picture themselves, but this request coincided with the return to the scene of Busby

With Frank Sinatra

Berkeley, and circumstances being what they were, Kelly and Donen agreed with Freed's decision to hire Berkeley. The once-mighty musical director had gone through several years of unemployment due to personal misfortunes and a nervous breakdown, and he came to Freed for help to reestablish himself. Freed was not unmindful of Berkeley's contribution to his own start as a producer, having directed *Babes in Arms* and *Strike Up the Band,* the first two Freed musicals, and four other films. However, despite the directorial credit of *Take Me Out to the Ball Game* going to Berkeley, most of the film's musical sequences were actually directed by Kelly and Donen, and it was this work that persuaded Freed to let them direct *On the Town.*

This is not a great musical, but it does have an easy flow, an amiable atmosphere, and some pleasant but not memorable songs. The plot concerns a popular song-and-dance team—Dennis Ryan (Sinatra) and Eddie O'Brien (Kelly)—who spend each summer as members of a baseball team called The Wolves. The members are anxiously awaiting the arrival of a new owner-manager, K. C. Higgins (Esther Williams), and they are amazed to find this person to be a pretty young woman. Both Dennis and Eddie are romantically attracted to the boss, but she shows them little interest other than in their ability to play baseball, and she turns out to be a tough employer. The ambitious Eddie can't resist an offer to spend his evenings directing a nightclub act, which causes him to be benched for breaking the rules of training, and he allows himself to get involved with a charming, flattering but crooked gambling czar, Joe Lorgan (Edward Arnold), who is scheming to wreck the Wolves in favor of his investment in an opposition club. Eddie unwittingly falls into this trap, until he realizes what is happening. Lorgan tries to keep him from playing in the major game of the season, but Eddie fights his way back to his team and helps them win the pennant. In doing so he also wins the affection of K. C. Higgins, whose friend Shirley (Betty Garrett) has finally managed to get Dennis's mind off the boss and aimed in her own amorous direction.

Aside from the five songs written for the picture, the film employs the famous ditty used as its title, which was written by Albert Von Tilzer and vaudevillian Jack Norworth in 1911—roughly the time period of this picture. For his solo Gene Kelly made his own choice of material, "The Hat My Father Wore on St. Patrick's Day," another vintage

With Esther Williams, Tom Dugan and Richard Lane

With Esther Williams and Tom Dugan

With director Busby Berkeley

With Richard Lane, Tom Dugan, and Jules Munshin

97

piece, and blatantly Irish in spite of its authors being identified as G. Schwartz and W. Jerome. As performed by Kelly, this is a typical shamrock-and-shillelagh rouser, pleasingly cocky and full of vigorous tap-stepping. Sinatra's solo is a gentle ballad, "The Right Girl for Me," and he and Betty Garrett sing a more vigorous version of the same sentiments in "It's Fate, Baby, It's Fate." Jules Munshin, as a genial, oafish ball player befriended by the two stars, joins them in singing the comic baseball number, "O'Brien to Ryan to Goldberg." Sinatra and Kelly also sing a ragtime ditty, "Yes, Indeedy." The finale, a flag-waver involving the whole cast, "Strictly U.S.A.," was written entirely by Roger Edens. It makes for a spirited wrap-up and steps out of the character of the film by making contemporary allusions in its lyrics, but such is the loose, unimportant nature of this musical that it hardly matters. The picture was obviously aimed by MGM at the summer trade.

Despite the general success of *Take Me Out to the Ball Game,* it proved to be the last film directed by Busby Berkeley. Luck was not with him on his return to the movies. He was next assigned to direct Judy Garland in *Annie Get Your Gun,* but although he and she had worked together in five successful pictures she now took a disliking to him.

With both of them in varying stages of ill health they were taken off the production after several weeks of painful frustrations. In the remainder of his career Berkeley worked as a sequence director in eight musicals, and with the gradual demise of movie musicals he virtually disappeared. It wasn't until the mid-sixties that he was justly heralded for his work as an inventive, highly imaginative devisor of cinematic musical material. Said Gene Kelly: "Buzz was probably the most remarkable talent the Hollywood musical ever had. More than anybody else he showed what could be done with a movie camera—and long before there was such a thing as a zoom lens or a helicopter. He tore away the proscenium arch for the movie musical and anyone interested in making films should study what Berkeley did, particularly in his Warner films of the thirties. Study the shots and the angles and the perpetual movement. Some of it looks a little gimmicky today, but remember that he was the pioneer of the fluid style. In the space of about five years he did everything with a camera that can be done. I was lucky to have him as my first director and I learned a lot from Buzz Berkeley, not the least of which was to keep my eyes open at all times in making films and to look for new ways to do things."

With Jules Munshin, Betty Garrett, Frank Sinatra, and Esther Williams

With Vera-Ellen

ON THE TOWN

CREDITS:

An MGM Production 1950. Produced by Arthur Freed. Directed by Gene Kelly and Stanley Donen. Screenplay by Betty Comden and Adolph Green, based on their musical play. Lyrics by Comden and Green, with music by Leonard Bernstein and additional music for the film by Roger Edens. Musical direction by Lennie Hayton. Photographed in Technicolor by Harold Rosson. Art direction by Cedric Gibbons and Jack Martin Smith. Edited by Ralph E. Winters. Running time: 97 minutes.

CAST:

Gabey: Gene Kelly; *Chip:* Frank Sinatra; *Brunhilde Esterhazy:* Betty Garrett; *Claire Huddesen:* Ann Miller; *Ozzie:* Jules Munshin; *Ivy Smith:* Vera-Ellen; *Mme. Dilyovska:* Florence Bates; *Lucy Shmeeler:* Alice Pearce; *Professor:* George Meader.

The Brooklyn Navy Yard early on a fine summer morning: a beefy dockworker ambles and yawns his way to his job singing "I feel like I'm not out of bed yet . . ." A time whistle blasts the air and the figures "6:00 A.M." appear on the screen. The camera cuts to a naval warship and it fairly explodes with sailors in white uniforms as they eagerly start a twenty-four-hour shore leave. Three of them rush toward the audience to exclaim, "New York, New York, it's a wonderful town . . ." and then proceed to spend a day proving their optimism to be well founded.

Thus the opening of *On the Town*, the most inventive and effervescent movie musical Hollywood had thus far produced and an important

99

With Frank Sinatra

With Frank Sinatra and Jules Munshin

The Dream Dance

With Frank Sinatra, Betty Garrett, Florence Bates, Jules Munshin and Ann Miller

With Alice Pearce

101

With Betty Garrett, Ann Miller, Jules Munshin, Frank Sinatra and Alice Pearce

one in that it opened up the form and led to more development of modern dancing on the screen and a greater use of locations. More than any other, it took the musical out of the studio and into life. The credit for this belongs to Gene Kelly; he undoubtedly was not the first man to think of it, but he was the first to persuade a studio to let him do it.

By 1949 Kelly was a man to be taken seriously at MGM; for some time he had been given a greater say in the choice and the staging of the dances in his films, and his desire to completely direct musicals was well known. With the powerful Arthur Freed as his champion, Kelly had the studio purchase the rights to the musical comedy, *On the Town,* with music by Leonard Bernstein and book and lyrics by Betty Comden and Adolph Green. This remarkable musical had been a ground-breaker in the theatre and Kelly was determined that it would do the same for the film medium. It began its life as *Fancy Free,* a modernistic ballet by Bernstein and choreographer Jerome Robbins, in which three sailors expressed their shore leave adventures in dances. This inspired Comden and Green, who were at this time performers in musical revues, to devise a comedic story around the same situation, and they presented it to director George Abbott. He immediately approved the idea and commissioned Comden and Green to write the book and the lyrics, with Bernstein supplying the music and Robbins the choreography.

The project developed very quickly, and *On the Town* made its debut December 28, 1944, barely half a year after *Fancy Free* had made its bow. In its happy fusion of songs, dances and dialogue it was hailed as a milestone in the American musical theatre. And in making it into a film, Gene Kelly fought MGM in order not to have to make it at the studio and to do the whole thing in New York. They compromised and Kelly was allowed one week on location. It is the footage gained in that one frantic week that gives this picture much of its sparkle.

The decision was made to drop most of the score of the original, which MGM believed would not be popular with moviegoers. Also, and this is the reason many stage musicals lost all but their hit numbers when made into films, the studio had its own publishing outlet and more money could be made assigning its staff composers to create new material. Comden and Green were contracted by MGM to write the screenplay and the lyrics for the new songs, with music by Roger Edens. Of the Bernstein original it was deemed necessary to retain the opening recitative and the "New York, New York" exposition song—veritably the theme of the show—and the music for the dances, "Miss Turnstiles" and "A Day in New York," plus one comic song "Come Up to My Place." Six new numbers were written.

The three sailors are Gabey (Kelly), Chip (Frank Sinatra) and Ozzie (Jules Munshin). They begin their day with a whirlwind tour of New York City, and the staging of this sequence is such that the audience sees a dozen locations in the space of a few minutes, with cut-shots matched to the tempo of the music and the flavor of the lyrics. They visit the Statue of Liberty, they prance through Rockefeller Center and scamper around Central Park. A big poster of a beautiful girl catches Gabey's eye— "Miss Turnstiles for June"—Ivy Smith (Vera-Ellen), the choice of the New York Subway System as the monthly symbol of all that is best in the American girl. As Gabey reads the virtues extolled by the poster he fantasizes and sees her in an elaborate ballet of various sports and gymnastics. Then a lady taxi driver comes into view, Brunhilde Esterhazy (Betty Garrett) and they hire her to take them to the Museum of Natural History. Brunhilde takes a fancy to Chip and joins the group. Inside the museum a lovely anthropological student, Claire Huddesen (Ann Miller) tells Ozzie, adoringly, that he has a face like a caveman. After making known her love of studying mankind, Claire launches into a merry song and tap-dance, "Prehistoric Man," which ends with the collapse of the rare bones of a huge dinosaur, causing the group to beat a fast retreat.

Chip and Ozzie have found loving female companionship but Gabey thinks only of Miss Turnstiles and how to locate her. Brunhilde makes her intentions obvious as she sings to Chip, "Come Up to My Place," but when she does get him up there she finds her homely roommate Lucy Schmeeler (Alice Pearce) unexpectedly at home nursing a nasty cold. But poor Lucy is persuaded to leave.

Meanwhile Gabey has wandered into Carnegie Hall. There, in an upper chamber, Ivy Smith is taking ballet lessons from a feisty old teacher,

With Frank Sinatra, Jules Munshin, Ann Miller and Betty Garrett

Madame Dilyovska (Florence Bates). Gabey introduces himself to Ivy and charms her into a date. He succeeds so well that she immediately joins him in a singing and dancing homage to American domesticity, "Main Street."

At about the same time Chip and Brunhilde are at the top of the Empire State Building, where he surrenders to her loving onslaught and croons to her, "You're Awful—Awful Nice to Be With." The other two couples join them and after baffling the policemen who have been warned to look out for the sailors who demolished the dinosaur, the six of them march away singing their intentions, "We're Going on the Town." They visit a string of crowded nightspots and find them all the same.

Suddenly, without explaining herself, Ivy disappears.

Ivy, it turns out, has a secret job as a cooch-dancer in a cheap Coney Island cabaret—to pay for her ballet lessons—and now, short a girl, Brunhilde offers Lucy as a substitute. He accepts, but every time a sailor heaves into view Gabey tries to hide Lucy's face so that it won't be known to the navy that he's had such a dowdy date. To cheer him up Lucy and the others sing, "You Can Count on Me," during which the impulsive Lucy gets carried away by her own passion and, with a tablecloth draped around her, she dances a sultry tango with Gabey. He sees her home and gives her a little kiss goodnight. Touchingly she says, "You bad boy. Now I won't wash that cheek for a year."

But Gabey yearns for his Ivy, and again his

With Frank Sinatra and Jules Munshin

Cavorting on Wall Street

mind-wanderings provide an inventive visual for the audience. "A Day in New York" is a surrealistic ballet in which the four other chums are represented by dancers, who join Gabey and Ivy in ensembles. The two principals express their love in a *pas de deux* and in a solo Gabey reacts joyfully to a billboard advertising Miss Turnstiles. This dreamy sequence fades and we are back to reality, with the three sailors and two girlfriends being pursued by the police for their museum damage.

They take refuge at Coney Island, where Gabey discovers Ivy at work. Embarrassed and tearful, she finds she has no cause to worry about the feelings of the adoring sailor. But the arrival of the police sends them all scattering, with the three gobs donning cooch-costumes and joining in the show. They appear in various guises, and as three veiled harem beauties they sing "Pearl of the Persian Sea." They even flirt with the cops but as Ozzie's skirt slips and his navy trousers come into view, the game is up. But the three girls plead with the police—to the tune of "Hearts and Flowers"—and the bewildered officers agree to let the lads get back to their ship, and just in time. The frantic twenty-four-hour leave comes to a close as Ivy, Claire and Brunhilde wave dockside farewells and

With Vera-Ellen

the three tired but happy sailors chant an undeniable "New York, New York, it's a Wonderful Town."

On the Town was budgeted at a reasonable $1,500,000 and a forty-six-day shooting schedule—remarkable in view of the amount of musical sequence and the complicated photography. The New York footage was taken in three shooting days and involved hidden cameras and much shoot-first-and-get-permission-later decisions. Photographer Harold Rosson achieved a difficult 360-degree turn in following the action of the players at the top of the RCA Building, and in the ensemble numbers dozens of camera angles appear in rapid succession—with credit to editor Ralph E. Winters. And as in every production on which he worked the musical direction of the late Lennie Hayton is superlative.

Roger Edens, who served as associate producer as well as composer, often said that the film would never had been made without Arthur Freed's sticking his neck out. The film was not liked by the MGM management when they first saw it, no doubt because it was such a departure from their formula, but they were proved wrong is assuming that it would flop. The result was a victory for Kelly and his co-directing colleague Stanley Donen. Donen worked mainly on the staging of the film, with the choreographic layout entirely left to Kelly. Said Edens: "Freed turned us loose on it. *On the Town* was a very happy wedding of creative spirits. Kelly is a worker—he loves to work. The whole thing was unforgettably exciting for us to put together." And according to Donen: "We had a five-week rehearsal period, and after four weeks we were ready to start shooting . . . we could have shot the picture backwards, we were so excited about the whole production."

New York was in its prime as a tourist attraction at the time of making this film, but the beauty of *On the Town* is not only the buoyant use of locations but the combination of reality with fantasy, the blending of the one with the other. It was also a giant step in the maturing process of the American musical, with songs and dances arising from characterizations and being used to advance plot. And doing it with pleasing exuberance. It is Gene Kelly's point of pride among his films. "I agree it may not be as good as *Singin' in the Rain* or as much of an achievement as *An American in Paris* but I think it meant more to the movies at that time. It's dated now, of course, because the techniques gradually became common

and the theme of sailors on a spree has been done to death, but in 1949 the idea of believable sailors dancing and singing in the streets of New York—using the city as a set—was new, and it paved the way for musicals like *West Side Story*. After *On the Town* musicals opened up."

On the Town has received a great deal of critical study and acclaim over the years but its case was very simply stated by British film historian Roger Manvell in his book, *The Film and the Public* (Penguin, 1955):

I do not know of any musical which pays higher dividends to anyone who sets out to enjoy it in detail. It bears seeing and reseeing for its speed, its subtlety, and its beautiful design, and for that particular kind of captivating American charm which it possesses in almost every sequence.

The dream ballet, with dancers substituting for Sinatra and Munshin

In Rockefeller Plaza

With Sinatra and Munshin on top of the RCA Building

THE BLACK HAND

CREDITS:

An MGM Production 1950. Produced by William H. Wright. Directed by Richard Thorpe. Screenplay by Luther Davis, based on a story by Leo Townsend. Photographed by Paul C. Vogel. Art direction by Cedric Gibbons and Gabriel Scognamillo. Edited by Irving Warburton. Musical score by Alberto Colombo. Running time: 92 minutes.

CAST:

Johnny Columbo: Gene Kelly; *Louis Lorelli:* J. Carrol Naish; *Isabella Gomboli:* Teresa Celli; *Caesar Xavier Serpi:* Marc Lawrence; *Carlo Sabballera:* Frank Puglia; *Captain Thompson:* Barry Kelly; *Benny Danetta:* Mario Siletti; *George Allani:* Carl Milletaire; *Roberto Columbo:* Peter Brocco; *Maria Columbo:* Eleaonora Mendelssohn; *Mrs. Danetta:* Grazia Narciso; *Moriani:* Maurice Samuels; *Judge:* Burk Symon; *Prosecutor:* Bert Freed; *Mrs. Sabballera:* Mimi Aguglia; *Bettini:* Baldo Minuti; *Pietro Riago:* Carlo Tricoli.

Having done nothing but musical and light comedic material for what he considered too long a stretch, Gene Kelly asked MGM for a straight dramatic vehicle. With the edited *On the Town* shaping up as a potential winner, he was in a position to have his wishes taken seriously, although the studio would have preferred to keep him in musicals. However, MGM ran themselves no risk in giving Kelly *The Black Hand,* a modestly budgeted crime melodrama almost certain to recoup its cost on their booking circuit. It did much more than that, being a tough little film with a strong point of view and excellent acting.

The Black Hand was a swipe at the Mafia, long before most people were made aware of that vast, nefarious organization by *The Godfather*. But the attack was cautious, localizing it to New York's Little Italy in the early years of this century and pinpointing a specific group of extortionists and terrorists known as The Black Hand. The film touched on the plight of many immigrants in these times of the great migrations from Europe to America, people who were to discover that the New World was not quite the bright fulfillment they had looked for. They were subject to the exploitation of American industrialists whose agents encouraged them to leave their homelands and thereby supply plentiful labor that helped industry control American wages, after which they were victimized by certain of their own people, of which the Black Handers were the most vivid example.

The film gets its momentum from the defiance of one man not to give in to the system. Johnny Columbo is a New York-born Italian youngster who is taken back to Italy by his mother when his lawyer father is murdered by gangsters for not complying with their demands. After his mother dies Johnny returns to New York, bent on vengeance, but he soon finds it impossible as an individual to gain any evidence or make any impression on other individuals in the Italian community to band together. The Black Handers have the situation firmly under control with their brutal beatings, bombings and kidnappings. Only when Johnny cooperates with police investigator Louis Lorelli (J. Carrol Naish) does he see signs of progress. He also finds his childhood sweetheart Isabella Gomboli (Teresa Celli) and her family are involved in the threats of the secret society, making him more determined to wage his campaign against them.

Columbo and Lorelli finally decide that the best way to gain evidence on the Black Handers is to examine police files in Italy. Lorelli considers it better that Johnny stays in New York while he himself goes to Naples. He there finds the evidence he needs, giving lists of gang members, and he mails this to Johnny, realizing it is too risky to carry it in person. But Lorelli is killed before he can leave Naples and the society seeks to discover the contents of the letter when it arrives in New York. A savage fight for the letter causes Johnny to be badly beaten and Isabella's young brother is held hostage by the society in order to keep Johnny from further action. But he finds out

With J. Carroll Naish

With J. Carrol Naish

With Teresa Celli

With Mario Siletti and J. Carrol Naish

where the boy is being held; he manages to blow up the headquarters of the Black Handers and gain possession of the incriminating list. The leaders are exposed and apprehended, and the vicious society—at least this portion of it—is brought to a halt.

The Black Hand is a neat, taut little picture excitingly directed by the veteran Richard Thorpe, and thoroughly convincing as a visualization of life in New York's Italian section several generations ago. MGM wisely sought a good deal of Italian talent in making the film. Gabriel Scognamillo, working under Cedric Gibbons, was responsible for the sets, and an appropriate score was written by Alberto Colombo. Many of the supporting cast were Italians, including leading lady Teresa Celli, whose Hollywood career unfortunately never went beyond this picture. The late J. Carrol Naish, a past master of national types, was superb as the police investigator, and Gene Kelly pleased his public and surprised a few critics with the intensity of his tough, ambitious Columbo. Kelly, a black Celt, thereafter had some problem persuading people he was not really an Italian.

With Teresa Celli and Barry Kelley

114

With Judy Garland (center) and Carleton Carpenter, with cigarette in mouth

SUMMER STOCK

CREDITS:

An MGM Production 1950. Produced by Joe Pasternak. Directed by Charles Walters. Screenplay by George Wells and Sy Gomberg. Photographed in Technicolor by Robert Planck. Art direction by Cedric Gibbons and Jack Martin Smith. Edited by Albert Akst. Songs by Harry Warren (music) and Mack Gordon (lyrics). Musical direction by John Green, with Saul Chaplin. Dances staged by Nick Castle. Running time: 108 minutes.

CAST:

Jane Falbury: Judy Garland; *Joe D. Ross:* Gene Kelly; *Orville Wingait:* Eddie Bracken; *Abigail Falbury:* Gloria De Haven; *Esme:* Marjorie Main; *Herb Blake:* Phil Silvers; *Jasper G. Wingait:* Ray Collins; *Sarah Higgins:* Nita Bieber; *Artie:* Carle-ton Carpenter; *Harrison I. Keith:* Hans Conreid.

Summer Stock was the last of Judy Garland's films for MGM, bringing her spectacular association with that studio to a premature and unhappy end. Until the making of *Easter Parade* in 1948, the public had had no reason to assume that Judy was anything other than secure in her private and professional life. But it now appeared she was bordering on nervous exhaustion and prone to emotional instability. These facts were made known to the management of MGM by her doctors, but the request for leave of absence was denied and she was instructed to proceed with her next assignment, *The Barkleys of Broadway*. Judy collapsed during the period of preproduction and she was replaced by Ginger Rogers. After convalescing she returned to do a short sequence in *Words and Music* and the lead in *In the Good Old*

With Judy Garland

With Judy Garland and Phil Silvers

With Phil Silvers

Summertime but it was obvious to those with whom she worked that the strain was too much for her. MGM had purchased the rights to *Annie Get Your Gun* with Judy in mind and insisted she do the picture, but after weeks of fights and problems she was suspended and sent to a clinic in Boston. Three months later she returned to start work in *Summer Stock*, now more plump than she had ever been and possessed with feelings of doubt. The filming stretched out over a period of eight months, more than twice its original schedule.

In his book *Easy the Hard Way* producer Joe Pasternak presents a sympathetic account of this period with Judy, explaining her inability to work and the sympathy given her by her fellow workers. Pasternak singles out Gene Kelly for his patience and his apparent willingness to spend as much time making the film as might be required. Like most of those who knew her well, Kelly is reluctant to discuss Judy Garland, "We loved her and we understood what she was going through, and I had every reason to be grateful for all the help she had given me."

As a movie musical, *Summer Stock* is a decided step back from the progress made by *On the Town*, being the kind of hokey show-biz yarn Judy Garland several times made with Mickey Rooney a few years previously. On the credit side it is pleasant, and it contains nine songs, all good and mostly up-beat. The story is elementary: Jane Falbury (Garland) is a young New England farmer struggling against odds to put her property on a profit-making basis, with the aid of her companion-housekeeper Esme (Marjorie Main) and local merchant Jasper G. Wingait (Ray Collins), whose son Orville (Eddie Bracken) is in love with Jane. Jane's sister Abigail (Gloria De Haven) is a would-be actress who persuades a theatrical company headed by Joe D. Ross (Kelly) to use Jane's barn as a summer theatre and live at the farm during rehearsals—without telling Jane. She at first resents the show people, disliking their conceit and boisterousness, but sensing she needs help around the farm, Joe offers his cast as laborers in return for the use of the premises. As time goes by Jane changes her opinions of the entertainers, she and Joe take a liking to each other that turns to love and, because of her fine singing voice, she accepts his offer to become the star of the show.

Summer Stock is, happily, almost all song and dance. It opens with Garland merrily singing in the shower, "If You Feel Like Singing"—which title was used for the British release of the film. Then, while driving her tractor across the fields she sings the equally optimistic, "Howdy Neighbor, Happy Harvest." As a song to admit their predicament in having to work for their keep, Kelly and Phil Silvers—again the slap-happy sidekick—sing "Dig-Dig-Dig-Dig for Your Supper." Gloria De Haven and Hans Conreid, as a ham actor, satirize old-fashioned musicals in "Memory Island," and a love-smitten Judy gazes at the heavens and sings "Friendly Star."

These five songs are the work of Harry Warren and Mack Gordon, but for the picture's main love song, "You, Wonderful You" the Warren melody has lyrics by Saul Chaplin and Jack Brooks. The melody is first heard as a background as Kelly tells Garland about his love of being an entertainer, leading into his singing the song to her and then doing a soft-shoe dance. This song is later used as a dramatically effective means of expressing his uncertainty, as he dances alone at night on a bare stage. The dance is built around Kelly's using the squeaky boards to motivate his moves and a sheet of spread newspaper as a platform for his footwork. This unique little dance was a Kelly invention whereas Nick Castle was the general dance director for the film.

The show-within-the-show allows for Garland and Kelly to perform a duet, "All for You," and Kelly and Phil Silvers to do a rollicking country-bumpkin routine, "Heavenly Music," in which they caterwaul their love of hillbilly songs, dressed in outlandish costumes with huge feet and end the number when their singing attracts a pack of dogs. Both this and the previous song were written by Saul Chaplin, who shared the musical direction of the film with John Green. For Garland's biggest solo number it was decided to use "Get Happy," the first hit song of Harold Arlen, with lyrics by Ted Koehler, dating from 1930.

Judy Garland's problems are not apparent in her work in *Summer Stock*. During production she was frequently late, sometimes failing to show up at all and at other times so doubting of her talent and the public's affection that she could not bring herself to perform. But once before the cameras, her professionalism gave her strength. Her dancing in this film is very good, particularly in a scene where a stuffy Historical Society dance is jazzed up by the theatrical troupe and Kelly inveigles Garland into a fast and furious "Portland Fancy." "Get Happy" was an afterthought by the studio, who felt the picture needed an extra wallop

With Phil Silvers

With Judy Garland and Gloria De Haven

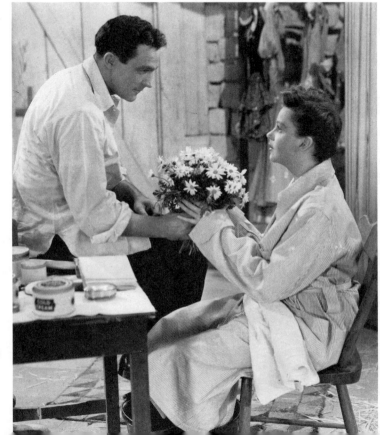

With Judy Garland

for the Garland fans, and it was filmed two months after the rest of the production had been completed—by which time she was twenty pounds lighter. The byplay between Garland and Kelly in this film is noticeably warm, but despite the excellence of her work and the continued interest of the public her health made her departure from MGM inevitable. Four years would elapse before Judy Garland made another film, and that would be for Warners, the magnificent *A Star is Born*.

With Phil Silvers

With Judy Garland

On the set with Phil Silvers, script clerk Les Martinson and director Charles Walters

With Leslie Caron

AN AMERICAN IN PARIS

CREDITS:

An MGM Production 1951. Produced by Arthur Freed. Directed by Vincente Minnelli. Screenplay by Alan Jay Lerner. Photographed in Technicolor by Alfred Gilks; ballet sequence photographed by John Alton. Art direction by Cedric Gibbons and Preston Ames. Edited by Adrienne Fazan. Music by George Gershwin, lyrics by Ira Gershwin. Musical direction by John Green, with Saul Chaplin. Choreography by Gene Kelly. Running time: 113 minutes.

CAST:

Jerry Mulligan: Gene Kelly; *Lise Bouvier:* Leslie Caron; *Adam Cook:* Oscar Levant; *Henri Baurel:* Georges Guetary; *Milo Roberts:* Nina Foch; *Georges Mattieu:* Eugene Borden; *Mathilde Mat-* *tieu:* Martha Bamattre; *Old Lady Dancer:* Mary Jones; *Therese:* Ann Codee; *Francois:* George Davis; *Tommy Baldwin:* Hayden Rorke; *John McDowd:* Paul Maxey; *Ben Macrow:* Dick Wessel.

Gene Kelly, Vincente Minnelli and others at MGM were concerned over the possible reaction of the French to *An American in Paris,* inasmuch as the French generally despise other people's depictions of their country. In this case they need not have worried; even the French Tourist Bureau could not have devised a sunnier glorification of Paris than this, so full of *joie de vivre.* But to be enjoyed it must be viewed for what it is: a pleasant fantasy barely related to reality. Except for a few establishing shots of Paris, the film was made on the sound stages and on the once-fabulous backlot in Culver City, and it is a purely American idealization of things French. Its great ballet sequence was designed in the style of several master painters, one of whom, Raoul Dufy, saw the film. Says Kelly: "I couldn't resist running it for him—but not without some feelings of trepidation. He was then a sick, very stout old gentleman in a wheelchair. When the lights went up we looked at him, afraid of what he might say, but he was sitting there with a smile on his face, tears in his eyes. He nodded his head at us and asked if we could run the ballet sequence again. With that we knew we would have no trouble in France."

The idea of the film sprang from producer Arthur Freed. He attended a concert with Ira Gershwin at which George Gershwin's tone poem "An American in Paris" was played. Freed mused that the title of the piece would make a good title for a film, and he asked the lyricist for permission to develop the idea. It grew to be an all-Gershwin musical, with Alan Jay Lerner hired to write a

With Oscar Levant

With Leslie Caron

With Georges Guetary, Oscar Levant and Mary Jones

With Leslie Caron

With Georges Guetary

With Mary Jones

simple story to link treatments of various Gershwin songs. For those with a liking for this composer, the film offers a generous sampling of his output, ranging from the early "Tra-La-La," written in 1922 for the Broadway show *For Goodness Sake*, to his last song, "Our Love Is Here to Stay," written for *The Goldwyn Follies* just a few weeks before his death in July of 1937. The choice of material was a group decision, with Vincente Minnelli clearly responsible for the inclusion of "By Strauss." He had been at a party in New York in 1936 and heard the Gershwin brothers kidding around with a parody on Viennese waltzes. Later that year Minnelli directed a stage musical, *The Show is On,* and persuaded the brothers to complete the material as a song for him to include in his musical, which they did.

The American of the title is an ex-G.I., Jerry Mulligan (Kelly), who has stayed on in Paris after the war to study painting. He lives in a tiny room in Montmarte, in the same building with an aspiring American concert pianist, Adam Cook (Oscar Levant), and the two seem to spend much of their time together at a nearby bistro, with the mordantly witty pianist unable to dampen the optimism of the lighthearted painter. Through Adam, Jerry strikes up a friendship with a successful singer, Henri Baurel (Georges Guetary) and offers his congratulations on his forthcoming marriage. His bride-to-be is a little girl he saved from the Germans during the war, Lise Bouvier (Leslie Caron).

Jerry's fortunes pick up when he himself is picked up by a rich, attractive American woman, Milo Roberts (Nina Foch) who promotes his career but fails to ignite any amour in his heart. The honest Jerry prefers not to be a kept man. Meanwhile, he—in a twist of fate familiar in the scripts of musical comedies—spots a lovely young girl in a nightclub and instantly falls in love with her. He pursues her and she rebuffs him, but Jerry is not to be deterred and when she finally agrees to keep a date with him, he learns she is the girl engaged to marry Henri. He attends the Beaux Arts Ball, as do Lise, Henri, Adam and Milo, but the festive atmosphere does nothing to lift Jerry's spirit, especially since he senses Lise now feels the same way about him. His mind drifts and he fantasizes about his predicament, touching off an elaborate imagination sequence. But Henri realizes the situation and releases Lise from the engagement—for a happy ending.

Slight as the story is, it serves as a reasonable

link between the many musical numbers, and the songs themselves occur at well-spaced intervals so as not to bombard the audience. The musical material is well tailored to the characterizations, so that although Kelly is supposed to be a painter, his expert dancing seems a logical expression of his personality and his feelings. The late Oscar Levant here appears in what is really a spinoff from his own career; the part allows for his spouting of barbed jests and much performing of Gershwin. The sequence in which he imagines himself at a concert playing the "Concerto in F," not only at the piano but playing the other instruments, conducting and being seen as members of the audience was his own idea. He had been asked to play a medley of Gershwin tunes but he objected and some time later came up with this suggestion. At other points in the picture he plays snatches of songs and accompanies Kelly in the joyful "Tra-La-La" in which the dancer hoofs around and on the piano. Levant plays and joins in the singing of "By Strauss" in the bistro, and although the piece is designed as a send-up of the Viennese waltz, it has the same lilt and gusto of its target. Another equally happy segment is Kelly's singing "I Got Rhythm" to a crowd of children on the street, leaping around to their amusement.

Georges Guetary, a popular French entertainer, made his only American film appearance in this picture and performed very agreeably with Kelly in a happy street duet, "S'Wonderful," and in a lavish theatre setting he sings "I'll Build a Stairway to Paradise." Leslie Caron, eighteen at the time, was hired for the film by Gene Kelly; he had seen her previously as a dancer with the Ballet des Champs Elysées in Paris and MGM accepted his word that she was right for the film. It was an auspicious debut. With "Embraceable You" as a background, she appears in a montage of different dance styles as the enamored hero images what kind of a girl she might be, and as a tender dance-duet he and she move to the strains of "Our Love is Here to Stay." They are also the principals in the fantasy-ballet.

The ballet sequence of *An American in Paris,* the most impressive thing of its kind ever used in a Hollywood film, was to have been shorter than it actually became. This seventeen-minute production ended up costing $450,000, and not a cent of it needed to be regretted. It was filmed after the rest of the picture had been completed, by which time it was obvious the studio had a highly probable winner in the works. Vincente Minnelli

With Nina Foch

123

With Leslie Caron

With Leslie Caron

125

worked with Kelly on the libretto and then left to spend five weeks directing *Father's Little Dividend* while Kelly rehearsed his dancers in his own choreography and a team of designers created the sets. Mention must be made of Preston Ames, the art director for this sequence. Ames had been a Beaux Arts student himself from 1927 to 1932, living in a Latin Quarter room similar to the kind depicted in this film, and he designed more than forty sets for *An American in Paris*, assigning skilled painters to recreate huge backdrops in the style of famed French artists. The backdrop for the Dufy-style Place de la Concorde was forty feet high by two hundred and twenty long.

Ames also designed the Beaux Arts Ball sequence and, at Minnelli's suggestion, fashioned it in a black and white motif in order to emotionally pre-

pare the audience for the bright colors of the following ballet. Gershwin's tone poem was re-orchestrated to improve the audio quality—he was not a first-class orchestrator at the time he wrote this (1928)—and a few minor changes were made in the structure of the piece, some deletions and extensions to suit the choreography.

The ballet begins as Kelly sits by himself on a balcony at the Beaux Arts Ball, ignoring the revelry inside, and looks out over the vast scene of Paris at night. His thoughts and his associations with the city and its painters materialize for the audience. Throughout the ballet he continually sees and courts and loses the girl, moving through familiar Parisian locations, all in the style of the painters who have influenced him. The Place de la Concorde swirls with people in a background suggestive of Dufy; he spots the girl and pursues her—through the Renoir-like streets around the

129

Madeleine flower market—through a gaudy fairground as Utrillo might have seen it—through the holiday throngs at the Jardins des Plantes, a favorite subject of Rousseau—and to the Place de L'Opéra, reflecting the art of Van Gogh, and finally to the Montmarte of Toulouse-Lautrec, where Kelly appears as the muscular white-tighted "Chocolat dansant dans le bar d'Achille," complete with Moulin Rouge can-can girls. Having made this whirlwind tour Kelly finds himself back at the Place de la Concorde, standing by the fountain, with all the people suddenly disappearing, leaving him alone looking at a red rose dropped by his elusive love.

This ballet is a summation of Gene Kelly's work as a film dancer and choreographer, allowing him his full range of style—classical ballet, modern ballet, Cohanesque hoofing, tapping, jitterbugging and sheer athletic expressionism. Kelly himself refers to his style as "a synthesis of old forms and new rhythms." He also wrote an article for *Dance Magazine* in which he touched on the problems of filming the *American in Paris* ballet: "We selected each artist's tone and 'felt' for similar tone in the passages of the Gershwin score. For example, that one brassy section could have meant

nothing else to us but Lautrec's "Chocolat" and we all agreed immediately that the "Walking Theme" was most potently related to the lightly sketched style of Raoul Dufy. Our chief trouble was with the Rousseau, which being simply primitive, seemed even more so against the score. But we felt that to omit him would be a kind of misrepresentation, so we made the 'American' tap-dance his way through a Fourth of July celebration in Cohanesque manner, against the theme of the music, while Parisian revelry spins itself out around his figure."

An American in Paris had the distinction of winning an Oscar as the best film of 1951, and six more for various contributions, plus a special Oscar for Gene Kelly by way of saluting his over-all work as a dancer-choreographer on the screen. John Green, who shared his Oscar with Saul Chaplin for their work in musical direction, says: "This was the team-job of all time, with Arthur Freed as its captain. Arthur was a real producer, an on-the-floor producer with impeccable musical taste. The whole thing was familial, and the Freed table in the MGM commissary was like the Golden Horseshoe at the Met. Both Gene and I look back on those years with Arthur Freed as among the richest of our lives."

The star, the director and the producer at their party at the close of production

With Janet Leigh

IT'S A BIG COUNTRY

CREDITS:

An MGM Production 1952. Produced by Robert Sisk. Directed by Richard Thorpe, John Sturges, Charles Vidor, Don Weis, Clarence Brown, William A. Wellman and Don Hartman. Written by William Ludwig, Helen Deutsch, George Wells, Allen Rivkin, Dorothy Kingsley, Dore Schary and Isobel Lennart. Photographed by John Alton, Ray June, William Mellor and Joseph Ruttenberg. Edited by Ben Lewis and Frederick Y. Smith. Musical direction by John Green. Running time: 88 minutes.

CAST:

Mrs. Brian P. Riordan: Ethel Barrymore; *Texas:* Gary Cooper; *Adam Burch:* Van Johnson; *Icarus Xenophon:* Gene Kelly; *Rosa Szabo:* Janet Leigh; *Papa Esposito:* Fredric March; *Professor:* William Powell; *Stefan Szabo:* S. Z. Sakall; *Mrs. Wrenley:* Marjorie Main; *Mr. Callaghan:* George Murphy; *Sgt. Maxie Klein:* Keefe Brasselle; *Mr. Stacey:* James Whitmore; *Michael Fraser:* Keenan Wynn; *Miss Coleman:* Nancy Davis; *Sexton:* Lewis Stone; *Secret Service Man:* Leon Ames.

Both as entertainment and propaganda *It's a Big Country* fell short of its lofty aims. This compendium of Americana, produced with obvious sincerity by MGM, smacked of sentiment gone somewhat awry; viewed more than twenty years later, in the light of so many changes in attitudes and lifestyle among Americans, it appears ludicrous. Its eight unrelated stories set out to examine America, and MGM lavished eight sets of actors, writers, directors, cameramen and composers to

With Janet Leigh

With Janet Leigh and S. Z. Sakall

With Janet Leigh

achieve an understanding and an appreciation of the various social and ethnic strata of life in the United States. It set out to do too much and resulted in too little.

The film begins with William Powell as a college professor lauding America to a dubious citizen played by James Whitmore, and this lecture acts as a springboard to a series of illustrations. Ethel Barrymore is seen as a dignified Bostonian lady angered at being overlooked by the census takers; then comes a tepid tribute to the role played by blacks in America; a young Greek-American (Gene Kelly) wins the love of a Hungarian-American (Janet Leigh) over the protests of her father (S. Z. Sakall); an army sergeant (Keefe Brasselle) delivers from Korea a letter to a stricken mother (Marjorie Main); a Texas cowboy (Gary Cooper) gives a tongue-in-cheek eulogy to his home state; a young Washington minister (Van Johnson) gets to meet the president; and an Italian-American (Fredric March) fumes at having to buy glasses for his son.

In the episode called "Rosita, the Rose" Gene Kelly appears as a breezy young man named Icarus Xenophon, who, because he comes from a Greek family, dislikes an old Hungarian store-keeper, Stefan Szabo (S. Z. Sakall), and the feeling of dislike is mutual. The two men are brought together when Icarus falls in love with Szabo's lovely daughter Rosa (Janet Leigh), to the approval of her impish little sister (Sharon McManus —the same youngster who danced with Kelly in *Anchors Aweigh*). This minor tale is amusing, with no strain on the talents of any of the actors. It was scripted by Isobel Lennart from a story by Claudia Cranston, and directed by Charles Vidor. But in showing how Cupid overcomes national prejudices in America, the episode can hardly be taken seriously.

With Janet Leigh and S. Z. Sakall

SINGIN' IN THE RAIN

CREDITS:

An MGM Production 1952. Produced by Arthur Freed. Directed by Gene Kelly and Stanley Donen. Screenplay by Betty Comden and Adolph Green. Photographed in Technicolor by Harold Rosson. Art direction by Cedric Gibbons and Randall Duell. Edited by Adrienne Fazan. Songs by Nacio Herb Brown (music) and Arthur Freed (lyrics). Musical direction by Lennie Hayton. Running time: 103 minutes.

CAST:

Don Lockwood: Gene Kelly; *Cosmo Brown:* Donald O'Connor; *Kathy Selden:* Debbie Reynolds; *Lina Lamont:* Jean Hagen; *R. F. Simpson:* Millard Mitchell; *Zelda Zanders:* Rita Moreno; *Roscoe Dexter:* Douglas Fowley; *Dancer:* Cyd Charisse; *Dora Bailey:* Madge Blake; *Rod:* King Donovan; *Phoebe Dinsmore:* Kathleen Freeman; *Diction Coach:* Bobby Watson; *Sid Phillips:* Tommy Farrell.

The track record of the late Arthur Freed as a producer is unlike that of any other in the history of films. He produced forty of MGM's celebrated musicals, starting with *Babes in Arms* in 1939, and the most autobiographical of them is *Singin' in the Rain.* The musical score of this picture is made up of songs Freed wrote with Nacio Herb Brown—indeed this is the cream of their catalogue—and the plot, dealing with the coming of sound to Hollywood, is an episode of movie history in which Freed himself was involved. He began as a pianist with a music publishing house and his work as a song plugger led to his be-

With Donald O'Connor and Debbie Reynolds

With Jean Hagen and Donald O'Connor

With Donald O'Connor, Douglas Fowley and Bill Lewin

With Jean Hagen

coming a performer in vaudeville. By the mid-1920s Freed was collaborating as a lyricist with composer Nacio Herb Brown, supplying songs for musical revues, and in 1929 they were hired by Irving Thalberg to write the songs for MGM's first musical, *Broadway Melody of 1929*, whose score included "You Were Meant for Me." They had written "Singin' in the Rain" in 1926 for a revue but it was also used in MGM's second musical, *Hollywood Revue*, performed by Cliff Edwards, Buster Keaton, Marion Davies, John Crawford, the Brox Sisters and George K. Arthur. Freed and Brown wrote songs for films all through the thirties, and in 1939 Louis B. Mayer contracted Freed as a producer, specifically to develop musical properties.

Plans took shape for *Singin' in the Rain* while Gene Kelly was still working on *An American in Paris*. The studio was anxious to keep the Freed unit at their happy fever pitch of creativity although no project had yet been hit upon as a successor to *American*. The idea of doing something about the early days of the movie musical and the panic caused by the switch from silence to sound germinated, and Betty Comden and Adolph Green were brought from New York to develop it. Says Kelly: "All we began with was a skit about a movie star becoming a sound star, and we all of us dashed around the studio asking the veterans what it was like in the old days and the script was built around the information we picked up. So what happened in the framework of the story was true, this is what it was like around MGM in 1928—with a little comedic exaggeration, of course."

Most Hollywood films about Hollywood have been cruel and strangely frank in exposing the sometimes shallow and vicious characters of its people, and although *Singin' in the Rain* is genial in its tone, its humor is still based on some rather unflattering observations of movie lore. It opens on a scene of tumult at a 1927 film premiere as a gushing Louella Parsons-type commentator greets the celebrated guests. The fans roar as the stars of the film arrive—Don Lockwood (Kelly) and Lina Lamont (Jean Hagen)—and after a few fatuous questions the commentator encourages Don to tell the story of his success.

What Don has to say about his early years is totally at variance with the truth, as we see he and his friend Cosmo Brown (Donald O'Connor) making unappreciated entertainment in tawdry burlesque houses and vaudeville theatre. Don tells

With Donald O'Connor and Bobby Watson

With Donald O'Connor

With Jean Hagen

of his coming to Hollywood and his immediate success, whereas the flashbacks reveal him as an extra who manages to persuade a tough director, Roscoe Dexter (Douglas Fowley) to let him be the butt of comedy stunts, which he does so well he catches the attention of a producer and becomes an actor.

Finally he gets to co-star with Lina Lamont, a none-too-bright beauty with an atrocious speaking voice. He feigns a romance with her to help his career, but Lina imagines he is serious. The egocentric actor doesn't become serious about love until he meets an aspiring entertainer, Kathy Selden (Debbie Reynolds). She rebuffs him, claiming to be a legitimate actress disdainful of the movies but this pose is revealed as false when she turns up as a chorus dancer at a Hollywood party. Needled by Don about this she retaliates by picking up a large iced cake and slinging it at him—but missing and hitting Lina in the face.

It is also at this party that the studio head, R. F. Simpson (Millard Mitchell) shows a new gadget, a short talking movie, but even Simpson doesn't believe it will affect the industry, "The Warner Brothers are making a whole talking picture with this gadget—*The Jazz Singer*. They'll lose their shirts." And Simpson's Monumental Pictures ploughs ahead with silent product. By now Don is more concerned about finding Kathy than pursuing his work and Cosmo does his best to cheer him up. Don proceeds with his new picture, *The Dueling Cavalier*, finding it harder and harder to be civil to the dumb Lina, but as they get into production we see *Variety* headlines telling us about the impact of sound and the revolution in the industry, followed by a montage of excerpts from musicals currently in production.

Kathy comes to the attention of Simpson, who vaguely recalls having seen her before, and he hires her. Don romances her and wins her approval, helped by his singing "You Were Meant for Me," but Lina blocks any plans for her success at the studio. Lina finds it painfully difficult to perform as a talking actress, driving her elocution coach almost mad, and when *The Dueling Cavalier* as a sound picture is sneak-previewed, the audience howls at the hideously bad pickup on the voices and the errors in synchronization.

The studio is about to scrap the picture when Cosmo has the brilliant idea of turning it into a musical and having Kathy dub Lina's voice. The result is a great success, and at the premiere of the picture Don pulls a trick that puts Lina in her place and assures Kathy her future in Hollywood. Asked to reprise one of the songs in the film for the live audience Lina agrees once she knows Kathy is behind the curtain at a microphone. But as Lina mouths the lyrics Don raises the curtain. . . .

This happy movie floats on music from beginning to end, with much of it used for dancing. Freed and Brown wrote one new song, "Make 'Em Laugh," to add to ten old ones and Comden and Green, with Roger Edens, wrote the "Moses" routine in which Kelly and O'Connor make a shambles of a diction teacher's attempts to improve their speech with tongue twisters. "Make 'Em Laugh" is O'Connor's impressive solo, a brilliant and frantic piece of comic dancing full of acrobatics and physical punishment. O'Connor also dances with Kelly and Reynolds in the sprightly "Good Mornin'" and performs several fleeting numbers with Kelly in the vaudevillian montage at the beginning of the film.

O'Connor here proved himself a major dancer. He was also supposed to have been in the film's largest production number, "Broadway Ballet," but a previous television commitment made it impossible for him to stay. This altered the original comedic intent of the number, causing Kelly to develop it into a sequence in which the hero explains to the studio head an idea he has for such a production in a film. The piece is built around two famous Freed-Brown songs, "Broadway Melody" and "Broadway Rhythm" and it was here that Kelly did the little bit of business that becomes almost a trademark—exuberantly chanting in staccato style, "Got-ta sing! Got-ta dance!"

The number tells of an eager young hoofer who comes to the Big Time and carves a career for himself. During one engagement a beautiful moll (Cyd Charisse) flirts with him but drops him when her gangster boyfriend flashes diamonds as a lure. Later, when the dancer is a star he sees her again and imagines himself dancing a love duet with her but when he actually approaches her she spurns him again. He shrugs his shoulders and the elaborate number ends with him seeing another youngster arrive on Broadway bent in the same direction.

This production, admirable though it is, lacks the cohesion of the ballet in *An American in Paris*. The "Broadway Ballet" was filmed after the rest of the picture, requiring a month of rehearsal and two weeks of shooting, and if it doesn't stand out quite as indelibly as Kelly intended it is simply because the uniform excellence of the entire film

With Kathleen Freeman, Jean Hagen and Douglas Fowley

With Carl Milletaire and Jean Hagen

With Donald O'Connor and Debbie Reynolds

doesn't allow for it. Fully sixty of the one hundred and three minutes of running time is taken up by the musical performances. Even the nonmusical performances are impressive, particularly Jean Hagen's horrible-voiced Lina.

The most memorable portion of *Singin' in the Rain* is the title number and Kelly claims it was the easiest of his major dances: "The concept was so simple I shied away from explaining it to the brass at the studio in case I couldn't make it sound worth doing. The real work for this one was done by the technicians who had to pipe two city blocks on the backlot with overhead sprays, and the poor cameraman who had to shoot through all that water. All I had to do was dance and the credit for that delightful little vamp theme which opens and closes the song goes to Roger Edens. My concern with this piece was making the action logical and we arrived at that by setting it up as you would a short story—with a beginning, a middle and an end. The reason for the dance is his happiness in winning the girl—the logic of his antics in the street is the expression of that happiness, and the conclusion is his being spotted by a policeman, snapping him out of his rapture. He then gives the umbrella to a passerby and walks away."

But it is the happiness of Kelly's dance in the rain that gives the piece its lasting life—that plus the lilt of the music and the simple declaration of the lyrics. The sight of a happy man skipping on the sidewalk, climbing a lamppost, letting a drainpipe of rainwater cascade on his face and jump around in puddles is a sight marvelous to behold.

Singin' in the Rain is probably the most popular of all Hollywood musicals, and a favorite subject for film students. Authors Betty Comden and Adolph Green tell of being treated like royalty in Paris by such esteemed filmmakers as François Truffaut and Alain Resnais because of their connection with *Chantons Sous la Pluie*. It rates

second in Gene Kelly's own assessment of his films, although he understands why most people prefer it to *On the Town*. But *Singin' in the Rain* is a testament to the talents of Arthur Freed, and, as Kelly says: "This was the golden age of the musical and it was largely due to Arthur. He knew talent and how to use it, what projects were best to do and which people were best to work on them. He was a nonpareil, and when I think back about all the people I had the good fortune to work with under his gentle command, I'm amazed. They were the finest."

With Debbie Reynolds

With Cyd Charisse

141

With Pier Angeli

THE DEVIL MAKES THREE

CREDITS:

An MGM Production 1952. Produced by Richard Goldstone. Directed by Andrew Marton. Screenplay by Jerry Davis, based on the story by Lawrence Bachmann. Photographed by Vaclav Vich. Art direction by Fritz Maurischat and Paul Markwitz. Edited by Ben Lewis. Musical score by Rudolph G. Kopp. Running time: 89 minutes.

CAST:

Capt. Jeff Eliot: Gene Kelly; *Wilhelmina Lehrt:* Pier Angeli; *Col. James Terry:* Richard Rober; *Lt. Parker:* Richard Egan; *Heisemann:* Claus Clausen; *Hansig:* Wilfred Seyferth; *Cabaret Singer:* Margot Hielscher; *Mrs. Keigler:* Annie Rosar; *Sergeant at Airport:* Harold Benedict; *Mr. Nolder:* Otto Gebuhr; *Mrs. Nolder:* Gertrud Wolle; *Keigler:* Heinrich Gretler; *Girl in Phone Booth:* Charlotte Flemming; *Lt. Farris:* Charles Gordon Howard; *Oberlitz:* Bum Kruger.

Decisions were made by Gene Kelly and MGM in December of 1951 which would affect the future course of his career. The enormous popularity of *Singin' in the Rain* and the high regard in which Kelly was now held in the industry should have resulted in an even greater degree of success but circumstances would prove otherwise. The American film industry was severely shaken by the impact of television, and the 1950s witnessed the deflation of many once-mighty careers. An unexpected casualty was the movie musical, totally unexpected in view of the brilliance that genre had reached, particularly at MGM. But that was not predictable when Kelly and his employers

With Richard Egan

With Pier Angeli and Austrian slap-dancers

In Salzburg, Kelly and Pier Angeli discuss a scene with director Andrew Marton

decided that he should leave for Europe early in 1952 and spend the next eighteen months making three films in succession abroad. There were two main reasons for this decision: to use MGM funds frozen in Europe, and to allow Kelly to benefit from a new income-tax ruling whereby the income of Americans who worked overseas for a period of not less than eighteen months would be tax-free. He had persuaded the studio to let him produce his dream-project, *Invitation to the Dance*, and he agreed to star in two nonmusicals, *The Devil Makes Three* and *Crest of the Wave*.

The Devil Makes Three was among the first American films to be made in postwar Germany, utilizing contemporary situations and taking a more compassionate view of the Germans. Films like *The Big Lift* (1950) and *The Desert Fox* (1951) encouraged a more enlightened attitude toward German problems and predicaments and *The Devil Makes Three* delves a little deeper in that spirit. Here, an American army captain, Jeff Eliot (Kelly) decides to spend a Christmas in Munich in order to seek out a German family who had sheltered him during the war. He discovers that the family died in an American air raid and that their daughter Wilhelmina (Pier Angeli) now works as a so-called hostess in a second-rate nightclub. Wilhelmina is bitter about Americans and generally disenchanted with life, but Eliot feels a sympathy for the girl that soon develops into love. Several people involved with the nightclub decide to take advantage of this situation, among them an effete singer-comic named Heisemann (Claus Clausen). Wilhelmina is instructed to use Eliot as a dupe in smuggling black-market items over the border into Austria. Actually it is Wilhelmina who is being duped—her bosses are Nazis smuggling gold in order to restore their party to power.

Army Intelligence is aware of this plot and Eliot is called in to be briefed by Col. James Terry (Richard Rober) and assigned to work on the situation with Lt. Parker (Richard Egan), which involves continuing his affair with Wilhelmina. Her feelings gradually soften toward him and although she still thinks little of the Americans, she makes it clear she loathes the Nazis. Eliot goes along with the smuggling ruse, but he is now primed and ready for trouble. He suddenly realizes the means by which the Nazis are moving their gold—the fenders of the car in which he is riding are solid gold. Before he can get this information back to the army, he and Wilhelmina are captured and

In Salzburg with Pier Angeli

sentenced to death, their demise to take place during a motorcycle race on ice. But Eliot overcomes the situation and takes after the Nazi leader, who turns out to be Heisemann. The chase ends in the ruins of the Adlerhorst, Hitler's former mansion in Berchtesgaden, and the Nazi loses the game.

The film remains of interest because of its location shooting in the Munich, Salzburg and Berchtesgaden of early 1952, and the scenes in the Adlerhorst are of especial interest because the ruins were later obliterated lest they become a tourist attraction. The winter landscapes work in favor of the melodramatics, the suspense and the chase, and the acting by the many German members of the cast is excellent. It is also amusing to note the American influence on the Germans at this time, with nightclub entertainers singing American songs in heavy accents and local youngsters jitterbugging, but there are a few moments of genuine native talent—some singing by the sultry Margot Hielscher and a little slap-dancing in Salzburg. *The Devil Makes Three* is at its best in its action sequences, which is not surprising in view of its director, Andrew Marton, who is famed for his staging of second-unit stunts, such as the chariot race in *Ben-Hur*, and the battles in *The Longest Day* and *Cleopatra*. Gene Kelly played his not very demanding role in a straightforward manner but the sad, beautiful Pier Angeli would have benefited from more sensitive direction than she received here.

With Pier Angeli

With Claus Clausen

With Pier Angeli

145

With Cyd Charisse

BRIGADOON

CREDITS:

An MGM Production 1954. Produced by Arthur Freed. Directed by Vincente Minnelli. Screenplay by Alan Jay Lerner, based on the musical play with book and lyrics by Lerner and music by Frederick Loewe. Photographed in CinemaScope and Ansco Color by Joseph Ruttenberg. Art direction by Cedric Gibbons and Preston Ames. Musical direction by John Green. Edited by Albert Akst. Running time: 108 minutes.

CAST:

Tommy Albright: Gene Kelly; *Jeff Douglas:* Van Johnson; *Fiona Campbell:* Cyd Charisse; *Jane Ashton:* Elaine Stewart; *Mr. Lundie:* Barry Jones; *Harry Beaton:* Hugh Laing; *Andrew Campbell:* Albert Sharpe; *Jean Campbell:* Virginia Bosier;

Charlie Chrisholm Dalrymple: Jimmy Thompson; *Archie Beaton:* Tudor Owen; *Angus:* Owen McGiveney; *Ann:* Dee Turnell; *Meg Brockie:* Dody Heath; *Sandy:* Eddie Quillan.

The pity of MGM's version of *Brigadoon* is that it was made in 1954, at a time when the public interest in musicals had passed its peak. This fall from favor caused the studio to economize, disastrously so in the case of *Brigadoon*. Gene Kelly and Vincente Minnelli had long wanted to make the film version, but legal rights were difficult to finalize. Their original conception called for the picture to be shot on location in Scotland, and to this end they scouted possible settings. After some time in Scotland it became apparent that the project would be defeated by weather, since it could not be relied upon at any time of the year.

146

They settled for shooting their exteriors in the California mountain country but that plan was quashed by the MGM front office, who insisted that the picture would have to be made entirely within the studio. It was also decided that *Brigadoon* would be photographed not in Technicolor but in Ansco Color and in CinemaScope. Few Hollywood directors have ever favored Cinema-Scope and in viewing this picture it is apparent that Minnelli was uncomfortable in his first encounter with the long rectangular frame. It would have been difficult to fill the frame with dancers and singers on location, but even harder in the confines of a studio.

Although *Brigadoon* easily lends itself to criticism, credit is particularly due art directors Cedric Gibbons and Preston Ames, especially the latter. Gibbons was head of MGM's magnificent art department, and his name appeared on every major production. Although he was entirely responsible for the settings of some pictures, he more often than not acted as a supervisor. For *Brigadoon* Ames did the next best thing to the actual location —he created a huge set that filled MGM's largest soundstage, devising it in such a manner that the cameras could shoot a full 360 degrees. This panorama was cleverly designed to give the illusion of great distances, in addition to which Ames built a spacious, attractive Scottish period village.

Brigadoon, the first of Lerner and Loewe's splendid musicals, dealt with fantasy, and for that reason had been a problem whenever it appeared in theatres. It first appeared on Broadway in the spring of 1947, to immediate acclaim, but it was thought from the very outset that it was a musical best suited for the film medium, with natural locations. Ironically, Lerner and Loewe suffered the same disappointment with *Camelot,* which Warner Bros. insisted on making on their backlot rather than in the fabled Arthurian areas of Wales.

No new material was added to the score for the film version, but several selections from the original were dropped. Admirers particularly resented the dropping of the songs "Come to Me, Bend to Me" and "There But for You Go I." Actually, both songs were recorded for the film and both are included in MGM's soundtrack album (E 3135) but they were deleted because they slowed the film. Kelly, ever doubtful about his singing voice, was not pleased with his rendition of the ballad "There But for You Go I" and readily agreed to it being cut. Greater accent was placed on the principal

characters than in the original; the most conspicuous casualty being the part of the soubrette, Meg Brockie, the village flirt, whose two lusty songs, "The Love of My Life" and "My Mother's Wedding Day" do not appear in the film, thereby reducing Meg to a bit part, but nicely played by Dody Heath. A more serious omission is "The Sword Dance," which formed an exciting part of the wedding ceremony in the original.

Brigadoon hangs on a slender thread—the magical possibility of a Scottish village long lost to history and coming to life once every hundred years for a single day. Two Americans hunting in the highlands, Tommy Albright and Jeff Douglas (Kelly and Van Johnson) lose their way in the misty countryside and stumble upon the village of Brigadoon on the very day of its reappearance. They find a happy community, full of people who can sing and dance, but they are puzzled by the costumes and manners, those of centuries ago. The two men assume it to be a carnival and surrender to its hospitality; Jeff enjoys himself at every turn but as the day goes by Tommy finds himself falling in love with Fiona Campbell (Cyd Charisse). She is romantic but cautious and sings about "Waitin' for My Dearie"—in a voice dubbed by Carol Richards—but as she feels more and more drawn to Tommy she joins him in singing and dancing on "The Heather on the Hill." Once he has won her love Tommy wanders through the village singing and dancing "Almost Like Being in Love." With a little rain it might match a previous Kelly routine.

With Van Johnson

With Van Johnson
and Cyd Charisse

With Van Johnson

With Cyd Charisse

The village of Brigadoon is in a festive mood over the marriage ceremony of Fiona's sister Jean (Virginia Bosier) to Charlie Chrisholm Dalrymple, who has previously let his intentions be known with the song "I'll Go Home with Bonnie Jean," a song so infectious that Jeff joins in the chorus. The happy occasion is marred by the appearance at the wedding of a jealous, menacing rival, Archie Beaton (Tudor Owen), who threatens to leave the village if the marriage takes place. By now Tommy and Jeff have learned from the schoolmaster, Mr. Lundie (Barry Jones) the story of Brigadoon, a village protected from the evils of the world due to the prayers of one of their former ministers, but with the provision that no villager may ever leave, since should anyone leave, the place will vanish forever. When the drunken Archie Beaton makes haste to escape, the Americans join the gathered clansmen in "The Chase," a spectacular sequence, excitingly scored with Loewe's music, rhythmically dramatic as the villagers run through the heather carrying torchlights. The chase ends with the ac-

With Van Johnson, Barry Jones
and Cyd Charisse

Confronting Hugh Laing

cidental death of Beaton. The village is saved
and the marriage proceeds, but Tommy realizes
he can neither take Fiona with him or stay.

Returning to New York, Tommy is reunited
with his fiancee, Jane Ashton (Elaine Stewart), but
he cannot get Fiona off his mind, or adjust himself to his old way of life. He makes the decision
to return to Scotland one evening in a swank but
noisy nightclub. In this, the most brilliantly directed sequence in the picture, Minnelli cunningly

With Van Johnson and Elaine Stewart

With Cyd Charisse

With Barry Jones

Rehearsing with Vincente Minnelli and Hugh Laing

Lining up a dance sequence with Jeanne Coyne and Vincente Minnelli

152

runs the banal chitchat a few frames out of sync, adding to Tommy's irritation and discontent. He resolves to return to Brigadoon, and such is the sincerity of his love for Fiona that the village reappears. She welcomes him and he becomes a part of the legend as they sing and dance "From This Day On."

Brigadoon was greeted as a disappointment by most critics and its impact at the box office was not great. This feeling of disappointment is common with many film treatments of stage musicals, few of which are constructed in a manner which allows for literal filming. The mood created between live performers and an audience in a theatre cannot be duplicated on the screen, and the material almost always needs adaptation, which often drains away some of the original charm and vitality. However, there is much to admire in the filmed *Brigadoon;* the musical arrangements and direction are faultless, as are the costumes of Irene Sharaff and the incredible accomplishment of art director Preston Ames. The performances are pleasing if not outstanding, and Kelly's choreography is sparkling in the Scottish group dances. His dances with the remarkable Cyd Charisse accent the theme of idyllic love in relatively simple balletic style and give the film its best moments.

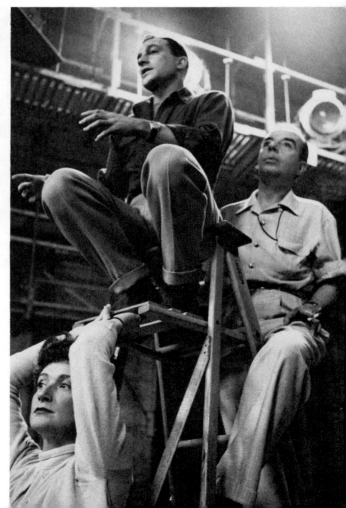

CREST OF THE WAVE

CREDITS:

An MGM Production 1954. Produced and Directed by John and Roy Boulting. Screenplay by Frank Harvey and Roy Boulting. Based on the play *Seagulls Over Sorrento* by Hugh Hastings. Photographed by Gilbert Taylor. Art direction by Alfred Junge. Edited by Max Benedict. Musical score by Miklos Rozsa. Running time: 92 minutes.

CAST:

Lieut. Bradville: Gene Kelly; *Lieut. Wharton:* John Justin; *Lofty Turner:* Bernard Lee; *Butch Clelland:* Jeff Richards; *Charlie Badger:* Sidney James; *Petty Officer Herbert:* Patric Doonan; *Sprog Sims:* Ray Jackson; *Shorty Karminsky:* Fredd Wayne; *Lt.-Commander Sinclair:* Patrick Barr; *Haggis Mackintosh:* David Orr.

Crest of the Wave is the American title for MGM's filming of the British stage play *Seagulls Over Sorrento;* the original title was kept for the British release of the picture. It was the first production of the Boulting Brothers, John and Roy, in their contract with MGM, although it is not at all typical of the kind of sophisticated satire with which they built their reputation. Recalls Gene Kelly, "I had seen several of the Boultings' movies and jumped at the chance to do the film when I learned they would be producing and directing it: It was a very deliberate hands-across-the-sea type project, to bolster Anglo-American sentiments and I was all in favor of that."

Seagulls Over Sorrento ran for over three years in the West End of London, but it failed to win similar favor on Broadway. It closed after only twelve performances in New York, the most obvious reason being its humor, much of it alien to

With Patrick Barr

With Sidney James

American ears, especially when spoken by working-class characters. This remained a minor problem in the film, although the story was enlarged and opened up for exterior settings. The main setting is a Royal Navy station on an island off the coast of Scotland, a remote location on which the Admiralty conduct research into new explosive devices for torpedoes.

The story begins with the death of a well-liked naval scientist in an unsuccessful attempt to solve the problems of detonation. Due to the lack of a similarly qualified expert in their own ranks the Admiralty bring in a U.S. Navy scientist to carry on the experimentation. Lt. Bradville (Gene Kelly) arrives with two American assistants, Butch Clelland (Jeff Richards) and Shorty Karminsky (Fredd Wayne), and despite the cordial British greeting there is an underlying resentment at the inclusion of the Americans in the project. This resentment provides both serious and comedic moments, with fairly conventional service characterizations in all ranks, British and American. The film breaks no new ground in this area; the serious differences are reserved for the officers and the comedic for the enlisted men.

Bradville's British counterpart, Lt. Wharton

With John Justin and Patrick Barr

With John Justin, Patrick Barr, Fredd Wayne and Jeff Richards

(John Justin) begins to resent the American when he sees him forging ahead with the work and bringing new ideas to it. Wharton fears Bradville will end up with the credit and rob his predecessor of due respect. The calm, cool Bradville does his best to allay these fears. On the enlisted level the British sailors resent the fact that the Americans don't come under the lash of an obnoxious R. N. petty officer (Patric Doonan), while they themselves suffer his tyranny. The station cook, Charlie Badger (Sidney James) is especially irate when he learns that one of the Americans has stolen the affections of his girlfriend. Through it all the commanding officer, Lt. Commander Sinclair (Patrick Barr) keeps the peace among his company of volunteers in the paternal, civilized manner long familiar in films dealing with the Royal Navy.

Tension increases when two British sailors die in yet another failure to detonate the experimental torpedo. Word is then received from the Admiralty to discontinue the project, but it is at this point that Wharton comes up with what he believes is the solution to the firing device. Rather than risk another man Bradville decides to take the torpedo to the test site himself. But he needs an assistant; lots are drawn to determine who he shall be. The winner is a genial British veteran, Lofty Turner (Bernard Lee), who cheats in the draw in order to save his colleagues. However, the test is a success and both men return safely.

Crest of the Wave is a neatly made film, as are most films made by the craftsmanlike Boulting brothers, and the performances of the British players defy criticism. Gene Kelly surprised a few critics with his restrained and plausible portrait of the naval scientist, carefully avoiding the air of mock heroism that might easily have spoiled the film. Asked by a journalist for a comment on Kelly shortly after the film had been completed, Roy Boulting said, "He's probably the most accomplished player I've worked with. He's absolutely sure of what he's doing."

With John Justin

With John Justin

With John Justin

155

Fred and Gene Kelly

DEEP IN MY HEART

CREDITS:

An MGM Production 1955. Produced by Roger Edens. Directed by Stanley Donen. Screenplay by Leonard Spigelgass, based on the book by Elliott Arnold. Photographed in EastmanColor by George Folsey. Art direction by Cedric Gibbons and Edward Carfagno. Edited by Adrienne Fazan. Musical direction by Adolph Deutsch. Running time: 130 minutes.

CAST:

Sigmund Romberg: Jose Ferrer; *Dorothy Donnelly:* Merle Oberon; *Anna Mueller:* Helen Traubel; *Lillian Romberg:* Doe Avedon; *J. J. Schubert:* Walter Pidgeon; *Florenz Ziegfeld:* Paul Henreid; *Gaby Deslys:* Tamara Toumanova; *Bert Townsend:* Paul Stewart; *Mrs. Harris:* Isobel Elsom;

Harold Butterfield: Douglas Fowley; *Berrison, Jr.: Berrison:* David Burns; *Ben Judson:* Jim Backus; Russ Tamblyn.

GUEST STARS: Rosemary Clooney, Gene and Fred Kelly, Jane Powell, Vic Damone, Ann Miller, William Olvis, Cyd Charisse, James Mitchell, Howard Keel, Tony Martin, and Joan Weldon.

Sigmund Romberg was a lilting and influential force in the American musical theatre for almost forty years, during which time he composed for some eighty revues, musical comedies and operettas. His total song output is thought to be somewhere in the region of two thousand. A film concept of his life and work was therefore not easy, but MGM acquired the rights to a very respectable book on Romberg by Elliott Arnold and put the project in the hands of two of the studio's major talents—Stanley Donen and Roger Edens. Donen had by now established himself as a director—his *Seven Brides for Seven Brothers* left no doubt about that—but the Romberg picture was Edens's first solo flight as a producer. He was for a long time Arthur Freed's right-hand man, writing lyrics, occasionally composing music, inventing musical sequences, and supervising production. His general role as a mainstay of Metro musicals has yet to be fully credited.

Deep in My Heart did better for Romberg than most other musicals about composers. The two hours of the film touched on sixteen of his songs and the production team astutely included some rare and unfamiliar material as well as obvious selections from *Maytime, The Desert Song,* and *The Student Prince.* To play Romberg MGM settled on Jose Ferrer, an actor with some knowledge of music and capable of musical performance. One of the highlights of the film is Ferrer's doing a frantic audition of the songs and the plotline of the show *Jazzadoo* for the backers in the space of just a few minutes. Another decided asset for the film was the casting of the late Helen Traubel, in her first film role, as Romberg's lifelong friend and booster, Anna Mueller. Miss Traubel at this time had only recently ended her lengthy association with the Metropolitan Opera, having acquired a reputation as America's foremost Wagnerian soprano and it came as a surprise to most people to find this very affable lady had a taste for light music. Her singing of Romberg's "Auf Wiedersehn" is nothing less than gorgeous.

With Donen and Edens making the picture, it was a certainty that Gene Kelly would be among the guest stars, but the selection of material was difficult in view of the limited range of his singing and the almost operatic quality of the Romberg songs. Donen and Edens solved the problem by digging into the composer's earliest work. Romberg arrived in America from Hungary in 1909 and earned his first money playing the piano in restaurants. and later leading small salon orchestras. By 1912 he was conducting his own orchestra at Bustanoby's Restaurant, and writing dance music, some of which was published. A year later he was hired by Broadway producer J. J. Shubert as a staff composer and set to work on a revue called *The Whirl of the World.* His next assignment was *Dancing Around,* starring Al Jolson, which appeared in the latter part of 1914 and told a tale of the British army in France. The song "It's a Long Way to Tipperary," written two years previ-

Jose Ferrer and Helen Traubel

On the set with his brother Fred and Ann Miller

ously, was interpolated in the score but among the many Romberg ditties was one called "I Love to Go Swimmin' With Wimmen." According to the film this was performed by a pair known as The O'Brien Brothers.

While "I Love to Go Swimmin' With Wimmen" is far from typical Romberg, it is, however, representative of the kind of music he was required to write in these Shubert shows at this time. It was not until 1917 that he was able to persuade Shubert to let him write the kind of music that interested him most—romantic, sentimental melodies. Hence *Maytime,* the first of his enduring operettas.

To perform the "Wimmen" number with him Gene called in his younger brother Fred, here making his only film appearance but who, before and since, had made a good living as a dance director in television and for stage shows. "Wimmen" called for no great skill from the Kelly brothers but it did require a lot of expended energy and boisterous clowning. The style is near-vaudevillian, the music is rapid ragtime and the lyrics contain couplets like: "I pretend that I'm a crab—and their pretty ankles grab," and "I get those navy notions when I see floating queens, I dive right in the ocean and play submarines." Assuming a taste for Sigmund Romberg, *Deep in My Heart* is a most enjoyable musical, and the love of the Kelly brothers for "swimmin' with wimmen" is one of its brightest segments.

Rehearsing with Fred

158

With Cyd Charisse

IT'S ALWAYS FAIR WEATHER

CREDITS:

An MGM Production 1955. Produced by Arthur Freed. Directed by Gene Kelly and Stanley Donen. Screenplay and lyrics by Betty Comden and Adolph Green. Music by Andre Previn. Photographed in CinemaScope and Eastman Color by Robert Bronner. Art direction by Cedric Gibbons and Arthur Lonergan. Edited by Adrienne Fazan. Running time: 102 minutes.

CAST:

Ted Riley: Gene Kelly; *Doug Hallerton:* Dan Dailey; *Jackie Leighton:* Cyd Charisse: *Madeline Bradville:* Dolores Gray; *Angie Valentine:* Michael Kidd; *Tim:* David Burns; *Charles Z. Culloran:* Jay C. Flippen; *Rocky:* Hal March.

The third of the celebrated trio of musicals directed by Gene Kelly and Stanley Donen, and written by Betty Comden and Adolph Green, *It's Always Fair Weather,* is admirable as a satire on commercial television and the advertising business, but in its appeal as popular entertainment it falls short of *On the Town* and *Singin' in the Rain.* The musical score of Andre Previn is a factor in point—it functions perfectly at every turn but it lacks the magic that turns a good melody into a touching and memorable melody. In this respect the gifted Previn is less fortunate than some of the songwriters who can barely play the piano. The idea of the film, a good one, was to bring together after an absence of ten years three wartime buddies and see how they feel about each other—a kind of sequel to *On the Town,* with the same trio of actors.

With Dan Dailey and Cyd Charisse

With Dan Dailey and Michael Kidd

With Michael Kidd and Dan Dailey

But things had changed, as much in Hollywood as in the lives of the characters in *It's Always Fair Weather*. Frank Sinatra had become more difficult with the years and MGM refused to deal with him. They also refused to accept Jules Munshin in a leading role, despite the efforts of Kelly and Donen. Dan Dailey met with immediate approval and for the third chum, the "little guy" role that would have been played by Sinatra, Kelly and Donen selected Michael Kidd, then held in high regard at MGM for his work as the choreographer of *Band Wagon* and Donen's *Seven Brides for Seven Brothers*. Thus with the selection of Dailey and Kidd, it was decided to build up the dancing in the film.

The film begins with an impressive montage, as we see three soldiers, Ted Riley (Kelly), Doug Hallerton (Dailey) and Angie Valentine (Kidd) making their way through the Second World War, ending with their marching into Tim's (David Burns) Bar on New York's Third Avenue to celebrate V-J Day. The merry warrior-buddies enjoy themselves and vow to meet in the very same bar in ten years' time. Ted is momentarily depressed when he reads a letter from his girl telling him the affair is over, but he puts the letter away and leads his chums in a bar-by-bar binge, dancing under the Third Avenue El, in and out of taxis and then, with garbage can lids attached to their shoes they thump-dance in the street. They depart after vowing eternal friendship with the song, "The Time Has Come for Parting."

Ten years pass and the three ex-comrades keep their rendezvous at Tim's Bar, each hesitant about it and doubting that the others will turn up. They greet each other warmly, but it soon becomes apparent that they are changed men and it is difficult to maintain the joviality. Ted in the intervening years has become a glib, card-sharp fight promoter of dubious ethics, Doug is a well-paid, stuffy, ulcer-ridden advertising executive and Angie runs a hamburger joint in Schenectady, pretentiously calling it "The Cordon Bleu." None of them has become what he hoped to be and their meeting only makes them feel uncomfortable as they realize their lack of self-respect. Their thoughts are revealed to the audience as the camera concentrates on each in turn and their alter egos sing verses of "Once Upon a Time." Too embarrassed to part they agree to have dinner together with Doug, the affluent one, picking an expensive restaurant. As they sit there together, munching celery and barely able to find anything to say, a string quartet

With Michael Kidd and Dan Dailey

in the restaurant plays "The Blue Danube" and their thoughts give voice to the strains of the Strauss waltz—"I shouldn't have come, dum-dum dum-dum . . . can these be the guys I once thought I could never live without?" The loud crunch of celery punctuates each verse in this trenchant little song.

Before the glum trio leave the restaurant a friend and fellow worker of Doug's, an idea girl in advertising, Jackie Leighton (Cyd Charisse) arrives and Ted makes a play for her. His glib technique makes little impression on the cool, intellectual girl but he impresses his work-place on her, Stillman's Gym, and she later turns up there, to the delight of a crowd of pugilists. She amazes them with her encyclopedic knowledge of boxing, and the ugly mugs are moved to sing a song in praise of their alma mater, Stillman's, the landmark of the boxing world, followed by a song in praise of Jackie, "Baby, You Knock Me Out," to which she dances her appreciation. Jackie also has a moralizing force on Ted, who knocks out his own fighter in order to prevent a fixed match. Meanwhile Doug goes through a similar soul-search and at a party of advertising executives he lampoons their absurd jargon in a wild room-wrecking song and dance, "Situation-Wise." Even Angie gets a hold on sanity and changes the name of "The Cordon Bleu" to "Angie's Place."

To speed his necessary departure from Stillman's Gym, in the face of retaliation from his crooked, fight-fixing rival Charles Z. Culloran (Jay C. Flippen), Ted puts on roller skates and makes off through the city. His mood brightens and he becomes his old, happy self again, and as he sails along the sidewalks beaming at people he sings "I Like Myself," following the vocal with nifty

With Michael Kidd and Dan Dailey

tap-dancing and skating figures. The roller skates give him a sense of release.

By now Jackie has learned the story of the three lads and has hit upon the idea of making them the surprise guests on the popular TV show, "Midnight with Madeleine." Madeleine Bradville (Dolores Gray) is a cloyingly sweet, but privately tough, singer-hostess on a nightly New York channel who reveals the lives of the "little people" and showers them with the gifts of her sponsors. Ted makes it known he and the others feel the show is shallow and the charity unwanted, but when he spots Culloran and his thugs entering the studio to get him, Ted realizes an opportunity and goads the unknowing Culloran into revealing his business before an open microphone. Jackie, in the control booth, instantly directs the cameramen to switch to Ted and Culloran, and the brawl which follows is telecast. The three chums whip the Culloran gang and proceed to Tim's Bar to celebrate—with the spirit of ten years ago, their lives

now changed for the better. Also changed is Jackie's opinion of Ted, and when she turns up at the bar Ted knows he's got himself a girl again.

It's Always Fair Weather did only fair business when it was first released, seemingly failing to strike much response with the audiences of the mid-fifties. Its satirical digs at advertising and television seem more pertinent today than then, since the pomposity, bathos and glibness of those media at their worst are even more apparent. The dancing in this film remains its greatest asset, not surprisingly so in view of Kelly's being joined by Dan Dailey and Michael Kidd. The pleasing Dailey is brilliant in his "Situation-Wise" and for a man who had not acted before, Kidd is remarkably good as little Angie, although as soon as he begins to dance it is obvious he is no meek, retiring nonentity. The street dance with the garbage can lids belongs in the select collection of great film choreography, and Kelly's routine on roller skates is amazing in its dexterity, especially in the ease of the tap-dancing. But skating is something Kelly had learned playing ice hockey as a boy, and he claims the tapping was not as difficult as it looks.

The Kelly-Donen direction merits one considerable comment of favor—their clever use of the CinemaScope screen in making it flexible and intimate, something that had escaped previous directors. The giant mail-box-slot shape was always a problem and here the directors hit upon the device of splitting the screen into sections during the passages where the three men soliloquize their thoughts in the restaurant, the photography highlighting the individual and blacking out the other portions of the screen. Kelly and Donen also split the screen into separate independent panels to stage dances showing the three men performing their versions of the same thematic material. And in the television studio brawl the directors employed the wide screen to advantage, showing the several areas of the melee through the windows of the control booth and then picking them up on three different monitors, with each TV screen occupying a third of the movie screen, and showing parallel or contrasting situations. These techniques, while they would never become common in the use of CinemaScope because of the complications and the added expense involved, would however be adopted and further developed by others. But it needs to be remembered that the pioneering was done by Gene Kelly and Stanley Donen in *It's Always Fair Weather*.

With Dan Dailey, Dolores Gray and Michael Kidd

With Michael Kidd, Dan Dailey and Cyd Charisse

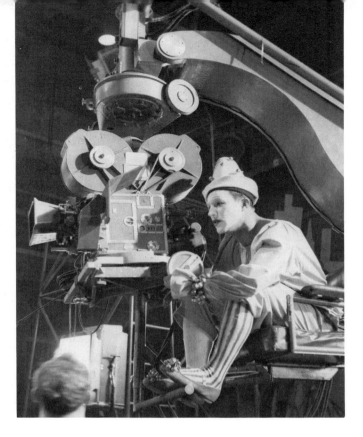

INVITATION
TO THE DANCE

CREDITS:

An MGM Production 1956. Produced by Arthur Freed. Script, direction and choreography by Gene Kelly. Photographed in Technicolor by F. A. Young and Joseph Ruttenberg. Edited by Raymond Poulton, Robert Watts and Adrienne Fazan. Running time: 93 minutes.

CIRCUS

CREDITS:

Music by Jacques Ibert, conducted by John Hollingsworth.

CAST:

The Lover: Igor Youskevitch; *The Loved:* Claire Sombert; *The Clown:* Gene Kelly.

RING AROUND
THE ROSY

CREDITS:

Music composed and conducted by Andre Previn. *The Husband:* David Paltenghi; *The Wife:* Daphne Dale; *The Artist:* Igor Youskevitch; *The Model:* Claude Bessy; *Flashy boyfriend:* Tommy

With Clarie Sombert

period of time. After the success of *On the Town*, which proved to MGM and the general film public that dancing could be used as a story-telling device, Kelly began to hound his employers for the chance to do a film that would consist entirely of dancing. They continually resisted the idea but with *An American in Paris*, and *Singin' in the Rain* to his credit Kelly became impossible to refuse. Recalls John Green, "Gene by now was the Neil Armstrong of MGM. He enjoyed great respect and admiration, and in Arthur Freed he had

Rall; *Debutante:* Belita; *The Crooner:* Irving Davies; *The Hat Check Girl:* Diane Adams; *The Marine:* Gene Kelly; *The Street Walker:* Tamara Toumanova.

SINBAD THE SAILOR

CREDITS:

Music of Rimsky-Korsakov (*Scheherazade*), adapted by Roger Edens and conducted by John Green. Cartoon sequences by Fred Quimby, William Hanna and Joseph Barbera.

CAST:

Scheherazade: Carol Haney; *The Genie:* David Kasday; *Sinbad:* Gene Kelly.

The most ambitious and the most personal of Gene Kelly's film creations is *Invitation to the Dance*, a full-length feature containing three ballets of various style but no dialogue and no singing. For Kelly it was a dream project realized only after much effort and persuasion over a long

164

a powerful ally. It was almost a father-son relationship, with the father having a near-reverence for the son. Also, Gene is not simply a persuasive man—he's a slugging persuader. There's very little velvet glove when he sets his sights on something, and so *Invitation to the Dance* came to be. Freed was nominal producer; it was Gene who determined the road map of the entire film, he sought out the talent, hired it, commissioned the music, devised the choreography, directed it and danced in each of the stories. It is *his* picture."

With Clarie Sombert

165

Having finally won consent, Kelly then embarked on what would turn out to be much longer and more painful then he imagined. MGM stipulated that the film had to be made in England at their Elstree studios in order to utilize frozen British earnings, and production began in October of 1952. Kelly originally conceived the film as having four parts, but the section to be known as "Dance Me a Song" was scrapped before it was completed because the material could not be realized to Kelly's liking. The idea was to have a group of dancers interpret a medley of familiar songs, arranged and conducted by Robert Farnon. The first section, "Circus," was danced to a score commissioned from Jacques Ibert, and it remains the best material in the film. The second section, "Ring Around the Rosy," a modern American ballet, was scored by British composer Malcolm Arnold but the MGM executives disliked his music and told Kelly to get another composer. This was an enormous problem because the same executives were not in favor of spending money to have the ballet refilmed. Andre Previn then performed the incredible feat of writing a score to a ballet already completely filmed to another man's music. Due to the great amount of time *Invitation to the Dance* had required of him, MGM instructed Kelly to proceed with *Crest of the Wave* before continuing with his ballet picture. By the time *Crest* was finished, MGM had decided that the final portion of *Invitation* involving animation, should be made in California, and so complicated were the requirements for that portion, "Sinbad the Sailor," that Kelly made *Brigadoon* while it was being planned.

"Circus" is a relatively simple ballet on a romantic theme, danced in classic style. In this Kelly appears as an eighteenth-century clown with an Italian traveling circus. The libretto is suggestive of *Pagliacci,* as the unhappy Clown reveals in mime his love for the troupe's leading lady (Claire Sombert), who is in love with The High Wire Walker (Igor Youskevitch). The troupe perform in the square of a village; tumblers, jugglers and harlequins create an entertainment that delights the villagers, but after the gaiety has subsided attention focuses on The Clown and it becomes apparent he is sad and lonely, and longing for The Girl. He watches as The Girl dances rapturously with The High Wire Walker. After they have gone The Clown picks up a cloak and dances with it as if he was a daring aerialist. The Girl notices him and in order to keep her

166

With Tamara Toumanova

With David Kasday

With his dance assistant, Carol Haney, who also played the part of Scheherazade in the "Sinbad the Sailor" segment

attention The Clown proceeds with amusing capers, ending with him climbing the aerial apparatus, from which he falls and dies. As he lies on the ground, a crumpled white figure on a red cloak, The Girl and The High Wire Walker realize the tragedy and resolve to love each other the more. The music of Ibert is excellent, fully stating all the joys and sorrows of the plot. "Circus" is Kelly's more serious film dance and he is well matched with Claire Sombert, a student in a ballet school when discovered by Kelly. For the role of The High Wire Walker Kelly says, "There was never any doubt in my mind who I wanted for that part, and I got him—Igor Youskevitch, the finest male classic dancer of the time."

"Ring Around the Rosy" is a takeoff on Arthur Schnitzler's story *Reigen* (*La Ronde*), in which a theme forms a link between a chain of lovers. In Schnitzler's tale the theme was syphilis—in Kelly's ballet it becomes a bracelet. The setting is contemporary American; the bracelet is a pawn passing between people of various kinds. A loving husband gives it to his wife, who gives it to an Artist, who gives it to one of his models. She passes it on to a flashy boyfriend, who uses it as a gift for a Debutante, who gives it to a Singer, and he bedecks the wrist of a Hat-Check Girl with it. A Marine (Kelly) takes it and gives it to a sultry Streetwalker (Tamara Toumanova), who returns it to the husband, who again gives it to his wife. The ballet begins and ends at parties, with other scenes at an artist's studio and on the street. The ten dancers perform a variety of styles, including tap and strong modern movements, as well as classic steps, in trying to set a sophisticated, racy tone to the piece. Previn's score, with him playing the prominent piano part, is suitably saucy and satirically paraphrases the nursery tune, "Ring Around the Rosy." The ballet is of interest to dance students, but lacks appeal for average moviegoers.

The final segment of *Invitation to the Dance* is the one which required the most work. In addition to Kelly and his assistants, the animation requirements of "Sinbad the Sailor" tied up some three dozen artists under the supervision of Fred Quimby, William Hanna and Joe Barbera of the MGM cartoon department for more than a year. A quarter of a million sketches were made to map out the sequence and 57,000 frames of film were painted to synchronize the cartoon characters with the live actors. The story depicts an American sailor (Kelly) on a shopping spree in Baghdad;

he buys an ancient oil lamp and after accidentally rubbing it with his sleeve a genie appears—not the monster usually attached to Aladdin's lamp but a cheerful young boy (David Kasday). The sailor first asks that the boy turn into a sailor like himself, and they then romp together through the pages of the Arabian Nights, with Scheherazade (Carol Haney) as their guide.

The two dance through a world of fantasy, through a valley of diamonds where they outstep serpents and then into the castle of a crooked Sultan, whose guards they elude. The pair foil the Sultan and steal away with his lovely, unwilling, bride-to-be. The lengthy sequence moves in a sprightly manner throughout, but some of the animation is overly cute. Critics were quick to point out that Kelly's results here were not as pleasing or as sharp as his animation sequence in *Anchors Aweigh*. Be that as it may, "Sinbad the Sailor" deserves credit for the sheer weight of effort and the courage it required to do it.

Invitation to the Dance fell far short of the mark Gene Kelly had aimed for. Work on the picture had been spread over three years, and, discouraged by the reactions at sneak previews, MGM held onto the film for another year before releasing it. The delay was costly, it was a case of the wrong picture at the wrong time. By the late fifties movie musicals were no longer the attraction they had been only a few years previously, either in America or Europe. Said Kelly: "When I originally set out to do the film, one of my chief reasons was the lack of filmed dance material available to the public, but in the space of four years that situation changed considerably. By 1956 people were seeing quite a lot of elaborate dancing on television variety shows, and there wasn't as much need for the film. And I must admit there were some things in it that didn't come off as well as I had hoped, although I feel "Circus" is really good. I also didn't want to appear in the film as much as I did, but this was at MGM's insistence. They were investing a million dollars and wanted some protection for their money. My name was about all they could gamble on. As a producer myself, I could see their point of view. And I tend to agree with those who find the whole thing a bit much—each piece is enjoyable by itself, but three in a row is probably more than most people can take."

While *Invitation to the Dance* must be judged an estimable failure it must also be recognized as an admirable piece of filmmaking on the part of a single man. No other entertainer has devoted as much time and effort in trying to interest the public in a movie about the skill and joy of dancing.

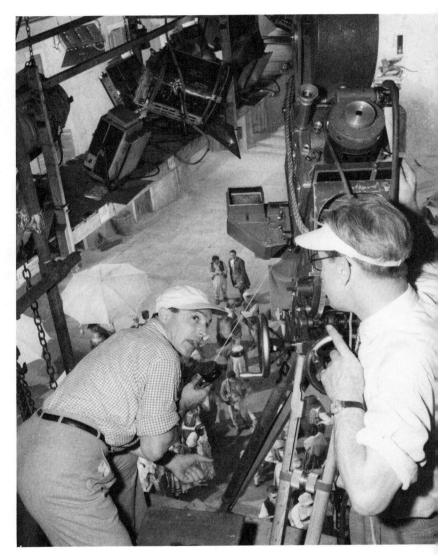

With ace British cinematographer Freddie Young

With Barbara Laage

THE HAPPY ROAD

CREDITS:

A Kerry Production, released by MGM 1957. Produced and directed by Gene Kelly. Written by Arthur Julian, Joseph Morhaim and Harry Kurnitz. Photographed by Robert Julliard. Art direction by Alexandre Trauner. Edited by Borys Lewin. Musical score by Georges Van Parys. Running time: 99 minutes.

CAST:

Mike Andrews: Gene Kelly; *Suzanne Duval:* Barbara Laage: *General Medworth:* Michael Redgrave; *Danny Andrews:* Bobby Clark; *Janine Duval:* Brigitte Fossey; *Docteur Solaise:* Roger Treville; *Helene:* Colette Dereal; *Morgan:* Jess Hahn; *Madame Fallere:* Maryse Martin; *Verbier:* Roger Saget; *French Motorcycle Officer:* Van Doude; *Patronne Hotel:* Claire Gerard; *Armbruster:* Colin Mann; *Bucheron:* Alexandre Rignault.

The Happy Road came about as the result of Gene Kelly wanting to terminate his contract with MGM: "I still had a couple of years to go but they had nothing on tap for me and I'd been sitting around for months waiting for an assignment. I couldn't stand not working so I suggested to them that we come to terms—that I do two more pictures to conclude the deal, provided they enter into a co-production with me on a property of my choice. They agreed to this, with the provision that I also played the lead, which I really didn't want to do because producing and directing plus being the star is too much. But at this point I was very eager to broaden my horizons."

Kelly had bought a script, partly because it was

set in France, where he was held in high regard, and partly because he knew it could be filmed on a modest scale. He set up a company, naming it Kerry after his daughter, and proceeded to Paris to organize his crew and his talent, with further time spent driving around France scouting locations. *The Happy Road* is yet another tale of an American in Paris, but not the cheery, foot-tapping kind Kelly had essayed just a few years previously. Mike Andrews (Kelly) is a brash businessman with little patience for the French manner of conducting business, which to him seems casual and inefficient. He is a widower and he has placed his son Danny (Bobby Clark) in a school in Switzerland. The ten-year-old boy feels his father looks upon him as unable to take care of himself and to prove otherwise he runs away from the school, in company with a female classmate, Janine Duval (Brigitte Fossey), who considers herself unappreciated by her divorced mother, Suzanne Duval (Barbara Laage).

The two youngsters set out for Paris and they are helped everywhere they go by children, who admire the pair for running away. The two parents join forces in the pursuit, with neither one caring much for the other because of their vastly different viewpoints. The failure of the French police to locate the runaways does nothing to increase Mike's feelings for the French, and when he comes across a British army unit on NATO maneuvers he appeals to the commanding officer, General Medworth (Michael Redgrave) for help. But Danny and Janine elude·even the military efforts to trace and trap them. After spending a night with a friendly woodcutter, the two youngsters get caught up with a European bicycle race bound for a Parisian finishing post and they hitch rides. Mike and Suzanne give up the chase and return to his apartment in Paris, where they find their two young escapees safe and soundly asleep. By this time the feelings of the parents have changed from hostility to appreciation, with Mike realizing there is something to be said for the French attitude to life and Suzanne feeling there is a lot to be said for this particular American.

The Happy Road suffers somewhat in overstating national characteristics, it labors the dubious point that children have better ideas on running the world than do adults, but the general feeling of the picture is warm and appealing and in several moments it is genuinely comic. Michael Redgrave gives a knowing send-up of a Blimpish British officer and numerous French character actors pop-

Directing Bobby Clark and Brigitte Fossey

Supervising a French barber cutting Brigitte Fossey's hair as her co-star Bobby Clark looks on

With Barbara Laage

With Van Doude and Barbara Laage

With Colin Mann, Michael Redgrave and Barbara Laage

ulate the picture with amusing bits of business. Barbara Laage is thoroughly believable as the mother, and if Kelly's playing of the father is more restrained than his usual performance it can only be that his mind was mainly on the numerous levels of his job as producer-director. He clearly recognized the slightness of his material and that the best way to treat it was briskly.

The well-photographed chase across France offers some pleasing shots of the countryside. But the point most to Kelly's credit in *The Happy Road* is his handling of his young actors, Bobby Clark and Brigitte Fossey. To find appealing youngsters capable of carrying a film is in itself a talent but to be able to sustain performances from them during the long weeks of filming is the mark of an exceptional director.

Gene Kelly's first film as a producer-director was made for slightly under half a million dollars. He took a small salary and a percentage of the profits, but the profits were few because MGM used it mostly as a companion feature on double bills and the bookkeeping on such arrangements is of a kind best left unchallenged here. But Kelly had proved himself totally responsible for the making of a film and that, as he had planned, altered the course of his career.

With Bobby Clark, Brigitte Fossey and Barbara Laage

172

With Kay Kendall, Taina Elg and Mitzi Gaynor

LES GIRLS

CREDITS:

An MGM Production 1957. Produced by Sol Siegel. Directed by George Cukor. Screenplay by John Patrick, based on a story by Vera Caspary. Photographed in CinemaScope and Metrocolor by Robert Surtees. Art direction by William A. Horning and Gene Allen. Edited by Ferris Webster. Songs by Cole Porter. Musical direction by Adolph Deutsch. Choreography by Jack Cole. Running time: 114 minutes.

CAST:

Barry Nichols: Gene Kelly; *Joy Henderson:* Mitzi Gaynor; *Lady Wren:* Kay Kendall; *Angele Ducros:* Taina Elg; *Pierre Ducros:* Jacques Bergerac; *Sir Gerald Wren:* Leslie Philips; *Judge:* Henry Daniell; *Sir Percy:* Patrick MacNee; *Mr. Outward:* Stephen Vercoe; *Associate Judge:* Philip Tonge.

Gene Kelly's final MGM musical has wit and quality, the script is superior to most others in this genre but the Kelly performance lacks something of the charm of his American painter in Paris, and the vitality of his sailor on a shore leave in New York. He was aware that this was his last performance for Metro, having accepted a directorial assignment as the second of the two items needed to close his contract, and that awareness subtly affects his playing. He declined to direct the choreography, and Jack Cole was given the assignment, although he was ill during part of the production period and Kelly took over in his absence. Cole Porter, whose last Hollywood score

173

With Mitzi Gaynor, Kay Kendall and Taina Elg

With Mitzi Gaynor

With Mitzi Gaynor, Taina Elg and Kay Kendall

With Mitzi Gaynor

With Mitzi Gaynor

this proved to be, later admitted he felt the script was good enough as a straight comedy and not really in need of songs, other than one for the variety act. But producer Sol Siegel and writer John Patrick, who had just worked with Porter on *High Society*, felt otherwise.

The ladies of the title are three singer-dancers: Joy, a level-headed, uncomplicated American (Mitzi Gaynor); Sybil, a delightfully scatterbrained Briton (Kay Kendall); and Angele, a temperamental French beauty (Taina Elg). They work for, and perform with, an American named Barry Nichols (Kelly) who tours with his nightclub act through Europe. Most of the story is told in flashbacks arising from testimony being given in a court case in London. Sybil, now Lady Wren, the wife of Sir Gerald Wren (Leslie Phillips), has published her memoirs and is being sued by Angele, now married to prominent French industrialist Pierre Ducros (Jacques Bergerac), for defamation of character. According to Sybil, Angele had attempted suicide after being spurned by Nichols but when Angele takes the stand she maintains this is not true and that Sybil was the one who tried to kill herself after being rejected by the boss. The Judge (Henry Daniell) warns the two respectable ladies that one of them is likely to be charged with perjury. Nichols appears on the third day of the trial to give his testimony—and solve the mystery. He declares that he was never in love with either girl and not responsible for their feelings toward him. His real interest among the girls was, and is, Joy and she is his wife. Nichols nonetheless defends the stand taken by both Sybil and Angele, explaining that they have told the truth as they understood it. He recalls arriving at the apartment shared by the two girls and finding them both unconscious as the result of escaping coal gas, an accident in an old, neglected heating apparatus and not the fault of either girl. The judge dismisses the case and the opposing parties embrace one another in an affectionate reunion.

The various pieces of testimony appear in the film à la *Rashomon*, as differing interpretations of the relative truth, and also serve to give the background of Nichols, his girls and their act. The title song is a snappy exposition number in which Nichols, backed by his three stunning employees, states the case for a happy song-and-dance man. The first line of the lyric tells us, "Round the map I've been a dancer, from New Jersey to Japan . . ." and then goes on to give the reason he most likes being a globe-trotting

With Kay Kendall

178

hoofer—working with beautiful girls. The three girls chime in with sentiments suggesting lusty approval.

The most memorable Porter song from this score is the gentle ballad, "Ça, C'Est L'Amour," sung by Taina Elg to Kelly in a little boat on a river, a situation which leads the girl to take seriously the lighthearted advances of her boss. The Finnish-born Miss Elg was a ballet dancer before working in movies and her ability is clear in her dance with Kelly, "The Rope Dance," a sensuous duet in a strange, geometric setting. The three girls appear in French period costume, circa Louis XIV, and sing a saucy ditty about their amorous duties as "Ladies-in-Waiting," and in a comedic dance routine with Mitzi Gaynor, Kelly turns up as a black-leather-jacketed motorcycle punk to sing "Why Am I So Gone About That Girl," an amusing takeoff on Marlon Brando's image in *The Wild One*. And in a typically Cole

With Kay Kendall

With Taina Elg, Kay Kendall, Mitzi Gaynor and Nestor Paiva

Porter joshing of upper-class love sentiments, Kelly and Kay Kendall sing and dance the sprightly "You're Just Too, Too!"

Les Girls was chosen as the Royal Command Film in London in November of 1957 and although it was thought likable most British critics considered it a slightly disappointing vehicle under the prestigious circumstances. But appreciation has grown for the picture over the years, recognizing it not only as the final Kelly-Metro musical but as one of the last films of its kind. By 1957 the Hollywood musical with an original script and score was getting to be a thing of the past,

partly due to a curious lack of impressive new talent to take over from the song-and-dance veterans—never a large group at any time—partly due to the public's saturation with musical fare on television, and the definite lack of popularity of original screen musicals in Europe. There was also the factor of cost, rising by the day, causing the studios to reason that the only kind of musical worth risking was one with a built-in reputation—the Broadway hit, but even in making films of famous stage musicals the results were more often than not disappointing. The talented and vivacious Mitzi Gaynor won the lead in the film version of *South Pacific* because of her performance in *Les Girls* but that multimillion-dollar production was a financial disaster and did little to further her career.

There are many enjoyable moments in *Les Girls* and most of them include Kay Kendall, in particular the scene in which she gets drunk on champagne and gives out with a raucous version of an aria from *Carmen*. Unfortunately she would appear in only two more films, *The Reluctant Debutante* and *Once More With Feeling*, dying in 1959 at the age of thirty-two, a victim of leukemia. Gene Kelly: "Kay was a delightful, charming, witty girl and that rarity of rarities—a funny, beautiful woman. Her death was a dumbfounding loss to everybody."

With Leslie Phillips and Jacques Bergerac

With Mitzi Gaynor, Key Kendall and Taina Elg

MARJORIE MORNINGSTAR

CREDITS:

A Beachwold Pictures Production for Warner Bros. 1958. Produced by Milton Sperling. Directed by Irving Rapper. Screenplay by Everett Freeman, based on the novel by Herman Wouk. Photographed in Warner Color by Harry Stradling. Art direction by Malcolm Bert. Edited by Folmar Blangsted. Musical score by Max Steiner. Song "A Very Precious Love" by Sammy Fain (music) and Paul Francis Webster (lyrics). Running time: 123 minutes.

CAST:

Noel Airman: Gene Kelly; *Margorie:* Natalie Wood; *Rose:* Claire Trevor; *Uncle Samson:* Ed Wynn; *Arnold:* Everett Sloane; *Wally:* Marty Milner; *Marsha:* Carolyn Jones; *Greech:* George Tobias; *Dr. David Harris:* Martin Balsam; *Lou Michaelson:* Jesse White; *Sandy Lamm:* Edward Byrnes; *Philip Berman:* Paul Picerni; *Puddles Podell:* Alan Reed; *Imogene:* Ruta Lee; *Carlos:* Edward Foster; *Karen:* Patricia Denise; *Seth:* Howard Best.

Herman Wouk's very popular novel *Marjorie Morningstar* was difficult to make into a film, partly because of its great length but more so because it dealt with a particular segment of American life, the upper-middle-class Jewish society of New York. In turning this into a glossy movie aimed at the widest possible audience Warners had to generalize the philosophy of its protagonists without losing the gist of the heroine's confusion, which is very much a result of her ambivalent attitude towards her background. This uncertainty of approach somewhat undermined the production of the film, with the studio management bothering the producer, the director and the writer all through the filming to popularize the material and avoid too precise a treatment of Jewish customs. By the end of production scenarist Everett Freeman was in favor of his name being removed from the credit titles, but he was persuaded otherwise. The long film, fairly entertaining on the whole, wavers in telling its story and it falls short of the sting and purpose of Wouk's book.

The girl of the title is eighteen-year-old Marjorie Morgenstern—uncertain of everything about her life. Marjorie (Natalie Wood) attends the Bar Mitzvah of her brother Seth, which occasion points to her spiritual doubts about the rigid religious views of her father (Everett Sloane) and her mother (Claire Trevor). Much more understanding is her genial Uncle Samson (Ed Wynn), in whom she confides her troubles. At Hunter College the stage-struck Marjorie receives applause for her perform-

ance in *Romeo and Juliet* and at the end of term she goes to Camp Tamarack in upstate New York as a drama counselor. In company with her saucy friend Marsha (Carolyn Jones), she takes a forbidden ride across the lake to visit South Wind, a resort complex complete with a theatrical company. It is there that she meets the dashing Noel Airman, singer, dancer, songwriter and director of the resort shows. She also meets his assistant, Wally (Marty Milner). He is soon smitten with Marjorie but she has no interest in him because she is dazzled by Noel. She and Marsha become part of the show and Uncle Samson, as a family spy, turns up to work in the kitchen. Noel accepts the love of Marjorie but makes it clear he has no interest in marriage. Her parents visit South Wind but they are unable to dissuade her from the affair with Noel. Uncle Samson, after giving a comic performance as a toreador for the resort customers, has a fatal heart attack and the grief-stricken

With Marty Milner and Natalie Wood

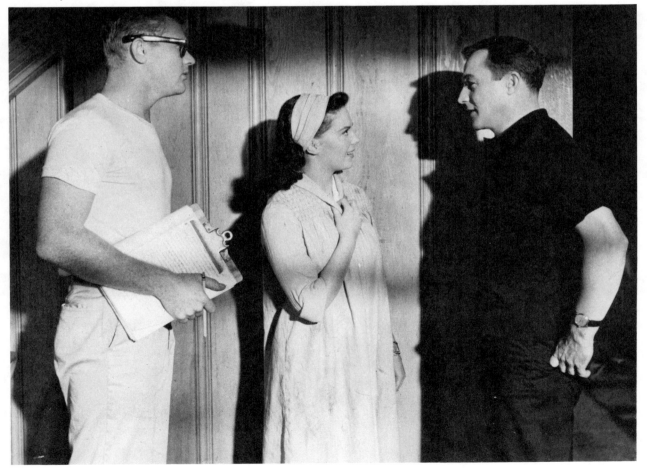

With Natalie Wood

186

Marjorie leaves South Wind. She decides to break with Noel and he understands. She takes with her the name he has invented for her, Morningstar instead of Morgenstern, having changed his own name from Ehreman to Airman.

Marjorie graduates from Hunter College the following year and it seems to her happy family that she will marry a respectable doctor, David Harris (Martin Balsam), but Noel reenters her life. Now in New York and employed by a Madison Avenue advertising agency, he tells Marjorie that because of her he has decided to give up the theatre and become a solid citizen, which causes Marjorie to fall even more deeply in love with him.

By this time Wally has become a successful playwright and Noel and Marjorie attend the opening night of his play. Noel, still show-biz at heart, is greatly upset by the triumph of his former assistant and he disappears. Marjorie locates him in Greenwich Village, sharing a room with a blonde, and walks away after slapping his face. Marsha, in the meantime, has become engaged to a theatrical producer, Lou Michaelson (Jesse White) and at their wedding Noel approaches Marjorie and tells her he is sorry and that he is working hard on a musical revue. Marjorie finds it impossible to ignore his need for her, and with her help Michaelson agrees to produce his show. Her parents are reconciled to the match and agree she should marry Noel. But the show is a flop and again Noel disappears. Marjorie trails him to Europe but in London Wally tells her, "Has it ever occurred to you that he doesn't want to be found?" He then tells her that Noel is back at South Wind. She goes there and finds him in his element, surrounded by admiring youngsters, and as she sees Noel escorting a young girl backstage she realizes the hopelessness of the situation. Marjorie returns to the ever-faithful Wally.

Marjorie Morningstar as a film seems to offer more comment on the psyche of those in the entertainment business than people of the Jewish faith. The title role, capably played by Natalie Wood, becomes the story of a girl of almost any background, adolescently rebelling against it, which is less than what Herman Wouk had in mind. His supposition, the anguish of repudiating religious and racial faith, not only affected the heroine but it explained the dilemma of Noel Airman, a Jew who had cut himself off from the stability of his background. It is his uneasy rootlessness, never fully apparent to himself, that sabo-

With Ed Wynn

With Patricia Denise and Natalie Wood

187

With Natalie Wood

With Carolyn Jones *(left)* and to the right, Marty Milner and
Natalie Wood

tages his confidence and causes him to drift—and finally retreat.

Danny Kaye was the first choice of Warners for Airman, an excellent choice in view of his own experience as an entertainer on the borscht circuit in the Catskills before his success on Broadway. But Kaye was diffident about the role, perhaps he understood it too well, and it was offered to Gene Kelly. Many consider this his finest dramatic performance and ne says, "I haven't liked all my roles, more often than not I wince when watching myself, but I had some good scenes in this one." A few critics mentioned that in playing a second-rate song-and-dance man Kelly's moments in the picture singing and dancing were too good for such a character, supposedly a summer-camp amateur. Explains Kelly: "Again this is a fault of the film treatment and not the book. Noel Airman is a very talented man, a brilliant fellow, the kind people think will take Broadway by storm. But he lacks either the guts or the drive, the ability or the confidence to push himself beyond the fringes of show business and take his place at the top. There are a lot of people like this. Wouk's concept of Airman was a valid one. Those who succeed in this business are not necessarily those with the most talent, but those with the most stamina and the most luck."

With Natalie Wood

With Doris Day, Gig Young and
Elisabeth Fraser

THE TUNNEL OF LOVE

CREDITS:

An MGM Production 1958. Produced by Joseph Fields and Martin Melcher. Directed by Gene Kelly. Screenplay by Joseph Fields, based on the play by Fields and Peter De Vries, and the novel by De Vries. Photographed in CinemaScope by Robert Bronner. Art direction by William A. Horning and Randall Duell. Edited by John McSweeney, Jr. Music: title song by Patty Fisher and Bob Roberts, and "Runaway, Skidaddle, Skidoo" by Ruth Roberts and Bill Katz, both sung by Doris Day. Running time: 98 minutes.

CAST:

Isolde Poole: Doris Day; *Augie Poole:* Richard Widmark; *Dick Pepper:* Gig Young; *Estelle Novick:* Gia Scala; *Alice Pepper:* Elisabeth Fraser;

Miss MacCracken: Elizabeth Wilson; *Actress:* Vikki Dougan; *Escort:* Doodles Weaver; *Day Motel Man:* Charles Wagenheim; *Night Motel Man:* Robert Williams; *Themselves:* Esquire Trio.

The Tunnel of Love was Gene Kelly's final movie in his contract with MGM. He was asked to direct the picture as part of the settlement which allowed him to close that contract prior to its original stipulations. Kelly readily accepted, he was looking for projects in order to solidify his reputation as a director and make known to the industry that this was the turn he wanted his career to take. The job was a pleasant one and Kelly claims the picture was shot fairly quickly and without problems, which no doubt accounts for the flowing good-natured mood of this glib sex comedy.

191

The film is almost a literal treatment of the play *The Tunnel of Love*, which opened on Broadway in February of 1957 and ran for more than a year. Joseph Fields directed the play, which he had written with Peter De Vries, and for the Hollywood version he both produced and wrote the screenplay. None of the leads in the Broadway original were called for the picture—the parts played by Tom Ewell, Nancy Olson and Darren McGavin went to Richard Widmark, Doris Day and Gig Young.

The Tunnel of Love was considered rather naughty in the late fifties, with its many titilating allusions to sex and risqué suggestions. Viewed in the light of later standards of permissiveness it seems almost quaint. It is largely a one-joke vehicle, the joke being the efforts of a childless young couple to acquire a child, either by natural methods or by adoption. The couple are Isolde and Augie Poole (Doris Day and Richard Wid-

mark) who finally apply to an agency for a child after giving up hope of having one of their own, but only after much, apparent effort that has left Augie gaunt and nervous and his wife hale and hearty. He is reduced almost to begging for mercy, and he is constantly needled by his neighbor, Dick Pepper (Gig Young), whose wife Alice (Elisabeth Fraser) is seemingly ever-pregnant. A representative of the adoption agency, Estelle Novick (Gia Scala) calls at their home, a recently converted farmhouse, at a time when the distraught Augie is walking around in his underwear worrying about mice. This does not give Estelle the impression he will make a fit father, and the situation is worsened by the appearance of Dick, who assumes the lady is a solicitor for a charity fund.

The main humor of *The Tunnel of Love* arises from Augie's efforts to win the approval of Estelle. He finds that away from her job she is

Doris Day and Richard Widmark

Richard Widmark, Gia Scala and Gig Young

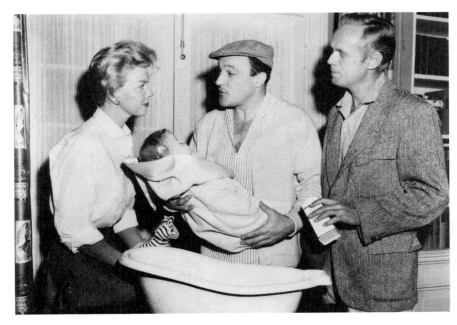

With Doris Day and Richard Widmark

With Gia Scala and Gig Young

quite cordial, and he plies her, and himself, with alcohol. But Augie is also on tranquilizers to calm his frazzled nerves, and the mixture of pills and drinks is too much for him. He awakens one morning in a motel room, alone, and not capable of remembering anything about his date with Estelle. Some time later she visits him to borrow a thousand dollars, explaining that she is pregnant. Estelle also tells him she will be able to arrange a child for him. Fearing the worst, Augie grows a moustache so that Isolde won't spot what he assumes will be a resemblance to the forthcoming child, which, to make matters more delicate, arrives nine months after Augie's date with Estelle. When the child arrives, a boy, he does indeed bear a resemblance to Augie, and Isolde threatens divorce. However, Estelle soon arrives to pay back the money she borrowed from Augie, and to show him a photograph of her newly born daughter and of her proud husband. Augie's great relief is then bolstered by Isolde's joyous news—she is pregnant.

The Tunnel of Love hovers on the brink of bad taste but the playing of the principals keeps it from falling. Most critics took a dim view of the film, claiming it to be falsely smutty, although *Variety* viewed it as being "without a snickering leer." Doris Day was here presented at her cheery, wholesome best and Gig Young played his flip, tippling gentleman in the style on which he must hold a patent. The casting of Richard Widmark did not seem to meet general favor with the public. Gene Kelly explains: "This is no criticism of Widmark, who is one of the finest film actors we have and who actually started his stage career playing light comedic parts. It's simply that the public fixes an impression of an actor, they accept him in a certain guise and they don't like him to stray too far from it. Widmark had established himself in serious material and they weren't prepared to accept him in this light, sexy part. The public creates type-casting, not the actors— unfortunately."

A dancing lesson for Doris Day as Richard Widmark looks on

Another dancing lesson for Doris Day and Elizabeth Fraser

195

INHERIT THE WIND

CREDITS:

A Stanley Kramer Production, released by United Artists 1960. Produced and directed by Stanley Kramer. Screenplay by Nathan E. Douglas and Harold Jacob Smith based on the play by Jerome Lawrence and Robert E. Lee. Photographed by Ernest Laszlo. Art direction by Rudolph Sternad. Edited by Frederic Knudtson. Musical score by Ernest Gold. Running time: 126 minutes.

CAST:

Henry Drummond: Spencer Tracy; *Matthew Harrison Brady:* Fredric March; *E. K. Hornbeck:* Gene Kelly; *Mrs. Brady:* Florence Eldridge; *Bertram T. Cates:* Dick York; *Rachel Brown:* Donna Anderson; *Judge:* Harry Morgan; *Davenport:* Elliott Reid; *Mayor:* Philip Coolidge; *Reverend Brown:* Claude Akins; *Meeker:* Paul Hartman; *Howard:* Jimmy Boyd; *Stebbins:* Noah Beery, Jr.; *Sillers:* Gordon Polk; *Dunlap:* Ray Teal; *Radio Announcer:* Norman Fell; *Mrs. Krebs:* Hope Summers; *Mrs. Stebbins:* Renee Godfrey.

Gene Kelly was vacationing in Greece when he received a telegram from Stanley Kramer offering him the role of the newspaperman in *Inherit the Wind.* Kelly was not immediately interested, being more concerned with finding film properties for production, but when he learned that Kramer had engaged Spencer Tracy and Fredric March to play the leads he changed his mind. "An actor need be dumb to turn down the opportunity to watch those two at work. I had known Spence through all the years at MGM and we often talked of doing something together, and I felt the same way

With Donna Anderson and Dick York

With Dick York and Spencer Tracy

about Freddie—veneration. It was a great experience just to be in the picture."

Inherit the Wind, both the stage play of 1955 and this slightly altered screen version, is based on the celebrated "monkey trial" which took place in Dayton, Tennessee in the summer of 1925. The trial was brought on by a biology teacher named John T. Scopes, in discussing Darwin's theory of evolution in a public school, contrary to the statutes of Tennessee. The film makes it appear that he was brought to trial as the result of bigoted public outrage, whereas in fact Scopes volunteered himself for trial in order to make a test case of the Tennessee statutes. The actual trial was conducted in an almost carnival atmosphere and was used for publicity purposes by its principals. The flamboyant Clarence Darrow, *the* lawyer of his day, volunteered, as did others, to defend Scopes, and the even more flamboyant politician William Jennings Bryan declared himself the apostle of

fundamentalist religion—truly a by-the-book man on every issue—and proceeded to speak for Tennessee. In addition, much of the controversy was artfully fanned and reported by journalist H. L. Mencken. For the film Darrow became Henry Drummond (Tracy), Bryan became Matthew Harrison Brady (March) and Mencken became E. K. Hornbeck (Kelly). The issues are idealized and the character of the two main figures somewhat softened, although the newspaperman remains a cynic.

As produced and directed by Stanley Kramer the film generates great sympathy for the teacher on trial, Bertram T. Cates (Dick York), in the face of spiteful prejudice from most of the townspeople, and most of its action takes place in the courtroom in a battle of wits and oratory between Drummond and Brady. The two men have long known each other, respecting their differences, and they seem to enjoy this epic platform. But as the trial drags on the feeling becomes more bitter

198

With Dick York and Spencer Tracy

With Donna Anderson, Dick York and Spencer Tracy

and less ethical, with the stoic Hornbeck quipping on the sidelines. Drummond becomes uncomfortable as he sees Brady bringing in thickheaded fundamentalist witnesses and refusing to accept Drummond's own presentations by scientists. Drummond is forced to make Brady appear ridiculous, laying open his narrow theories and

Fredric March

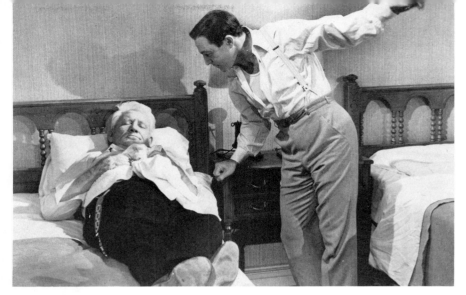

With Spencer Tracy

his apparent belief that his own interpretation of the bible is irrefutable. Cates is ultimately found guilty, but the evidence is such that the fair-minded judge levies only a token fine. Fearing that he has in fact been defeated, Brady launches into a frantic, babbling oration on his views, and as the people turn away his anger brings on a fatal heart attack. Hornbeck makes a flip, derogatory comment and finds himself blasted by Drummond for his cheap humor, his lack of compassion and his failure to grant that Brady had the right to his opinion.

The film is a credit to Stanley Kramer, a filmmaker with a penchant for tackling weighty, social themes. This has brought him adverse comment from the more captious critics but *Inherit the Wind* needs no defending. It is intellectually and emotionally stimulating in its dramatic discourse on the conflict of ancient and new interpretations of religious theory, and in the magnificent performances of Spencer Tracy and Fredric March it is a showcase for the art of acting. Some critics hastened to comment that Gene Kelly was miscast, but without explaining why. His Hornbeck is, in fact, precisely what the script calls for—a superficially amusing, hardhearted and somewhat lost soul.

Kelly's appearance in the film was due entirely to producer-director Stanley Kramer, who cast the picture with precisely the actors he wanted: "I've always thought Gene Kelly was a wonderfully sensitive actor. He had a sharply satirical quality in *Pal Joey* on the stage and he seemed a natural choice for a character based on Mencken in *Inherit the Wind.*"

203

With Marilyn Monroe and Yves Montand

LET'S MAKE LOVE

CREDITS:

A 20th Century-Fox Production 1960. Produced by Jerry Wald. Directed by George Cukor. Screenplay by Norman Krasna, with additional material by Hal Kantor. Photographed in CinemaScope and De Luxe Color by Daniel L. Fapp. Art direction by Lyle R. Wheeler and Gene Allen. Edited by David Bretherton. Musical direction by Lionel Newman. Songs by Sammy Cahn (lyrics) and Jimmy Van Heusen (music). Choreography by Jack Cole. Running time: 118 minutes.

CAST:

Amanda Dell: Marilyn Monroe; *Jean-Marc Clement:* Yves Montand; *Howard Coffman:* Tony Randall; *Tony Danton:* Frankie Vaughan; *John*

Wales: Wilfred Hyde White; *Oliver Burton:* David Burns; *Dave Kerry:* Michael David; *Lily Nyles:* Mara Lynn; *Abe Miller:* Dennis King, Jr.; *Lamont:* Joe Besser; *Miss Manders:* Madge Kennedy.

GUEST STARS: Milton Berle, Bing Crosby and Gene Kelly.

As originally conceived, *Let's Make Love* was to have been a satire on Howard Hughes, with the title *The Billionaire* and Gregory Peck in the leading role. After much deliberation with the legal department at 20th Century-Fox, the producer, the late Jerry Wald, and scenarist Norman Krasna decided to soften the attack by making the subject an international playboy-tycoon and to give the picture a title more in keeping with the charms of its very female star, Marilyn Monroe.

With Yves Montand

With Yves Montand

Yves Montand was chosen to play the part of Jean-Marc Clement, a New York-based French businessman of enormous wealth and power.

Let's Make Love assumes that a man like Jean-Marc Clement would take legal action if he learned a theatrical company was in the process of satirizing him—a fair assumption in view of the Fox lawyers' qualms about the original script. First, he decides to take a look at the show in rehearsal. He and his public relations officer, Howard Coffman (Tony Randall), sneak into the theatre to watch the actors. Clement's wrath melts once he sets eyes on the star of the show, Amanda Dell (Marilyn Monroe), a voluptuous, husky-voiced blonde who sings "My Heart Belongs to Daddy" as if she were a cross between Mae West and Shirley Temple. So smitten is Clement with Amanda that he allows himself to be mistaken for an unemployed actor and accepts an offer to be in the show. He orders his attorney, John Wales (Wilfred Hyde White), to purchase fifty-one percent of the show, and he hires the likes of Bing Crosby, Gene Kelly and Milton Berle for a crash course in singing, dancing and comedy. Amanda expresses contempt for the real Clement while growing

205

fonder of the man she believes to be an actor. Eventually he confesses his ruse and manages to persuade her he is not the ogre she thought him to be.

The film is uneven and not entirely credible but it does have many amusing moments, particularly those in which Crosby, Kelly and Berle labor to turn Clement into an entertainer. The sexy Marilyn appears to stunning advantage, especially in her Lolita-like opening "Daddy" number, and the talented Montand manages to play down his own ability as a song and dance man in portraying the superwealthy tycoon. Gene Kelly spent exactly one day doing his bit in the picture: "I'd long before promised Jerry Wald I'd do it but by the time they got around to shooting it I was in Paris lining up *Gigot*. He telephoned me, so I got on a plane and flew over the Pole to Los Angeles. Jerry met me in the evening at the airport; we filmed the next day and then he returned me to the airport. Would that all my jobs had been so well arranged!"

With Montand and Wilfred Hyde White

During a break with Marilyn Monroe and Yves Montand

With Jackie Gleason

GIGOT

CREDITS:

A Seven Arts Production, released by 20th Century-Fox 1962. Produced by Kenneth Hyman. Directed by Gene Kelly. Screenplay by John Patrick, based on a story by Jackie Gleason. Photographed in De Luxe Color by Jean Bourgoin. Art direction by Auguste Capelier. Edited by Roger Dwyre. Musical score by Jackie Gleason, arranged and conducted by Michel Magne. Running time: 104 minutes.

CAST:

Gigot: Jackie Gleason; *Colette:* Katherine Kath; *Madame Brigitte:* Gabrielle Dorziat; *Gaston:* Jean Lefebvre; *Jean:* Jacques Marin; *Alphonse:* Albert Remy; *Lucille Duval:* Yvonne Constant; *Madame Greuze:* Germaine Delbat; *Bistro Proprietor:* Albert Dinan; *Nicole:* Diane Gardner.

Films sometimes fail for reasons other than inferior workmanship and poor material. Often, with the best talent and the best of intentions, the picture doesn't jell—and *Gigot* is a sad case in point. Its star, Jackie Gleason, can be described as gifted rather than merely talented, and the work of director Gene Kelly and scriptwriter John Patrick need no defending. The color filming in Paris is delightful and the acting of a large selection of veteran French character actors is faultless. Despite all this the film was a flop, it drew few customers, and most of those who saw it didn't like it.

Gigot is entirely the creation of Jackie Gleason, his invented character, his performance, his musical scoring. The film grew, in reverse of the usual procedure, from Gleason's musical sketches of the character he had in mind. Gleason, an avid composer and conductor, hit upon the idea while engaged in one of his hobbies—sitting at the elec-

Jackie Gleason

tric organ at his home in Peekskill, New York, and improvising. *Gigot* is also an enlargement on a character often played by Gleason on television, his Poor Soul, a gentle oaf at odds with the world. He roughed out his plot and then hired playwright John Patrick, author of *The Hasty Heart* and *The Teahouse of the August Moon*, to expand it into a screenplay. With this in hand Gleason approached, because of his rapport with the French, Kelly to direct, and the two of them were able to persuade Seven Arts to back the project.

The film is more a character study than a story. Gigot (Gleason) is a mute and a simpleton, but a very warmhearted and genial soul who befriends children and animals, and receives little more than amused tolerance from local adults. He is employed as a janitor in a cheap boarding-house in Montmartre and lives in a dingy little room in the basement. Ever lonely, he ambles around the neighborhood longing to be accepted but the closest he comes to contact with people is when they take advantage of him and make him the butt of jokes. Gigot attends every funeral he can because in being a mourner he feels he can, for a little while, belong to a group of people. One evening he comes across a dejected prostitute, Colette (Katherine Kath), and her small daughter Nicole (Diane Gardner) and befriends them, taking them to his hovel to share his roof. He grows fond of the child, to the annoyance of the mother, who threatens to leave unless he can give her some money, which he then steals from a local baker.

Colette returns home one morning after a night with a client and finds Gigot and Nicole missing. She assumes he has kidnaped the child and alarms the neighborhood to that belief. Actually he is amusing the child in a cellar of the boarding-house, playing records and dancing for her. But the ceiling collapses on them and Nicole is injured. Gigot, full of anguish, carries the child to a church, where the priest summons a doctor. On the way back to his home to get the phonograph for Nicole, Gigot is spotted by the locals and they give chase. He escapes them but in doing so he falls into the Seine. They see his hat floating in the river and assume that he has drowned. Now filled with sorrow at the passing of the big mute, they hold a funeral service for him—and from a distance an appreciative Gigot watches with tears in his eyes.

The critical consensus was that *Gigot* was admirable in concept and a disaster in construction, and many seemed eager to point out that Gleason had aped Charlie Chaplin's silent little tramp and fallen short of the mark. Gleason, whose gift for mimicry is close to genius, was bitterly disappointed with the attitude of Seven Arts and 20th Century-Fox, who disliked the original finished version of the film and took it upon themselves to edit and change it. Says Gene Kelly: "This was

With Jackie Gleason

With Diane Gardner

During a break with Jackie
Gleason and Diane Gardner

With Jackie Gleason and visitor Brigitte Bardot

my unhappiest experience in the picture business. Our whole idea in making *Gigot* was to accent life in a community, to show its flavor, with the mute as the centrifugal figure. We showed the film to the armed services at camps in Europe and received enthusiastic response. When next I saw the film in New York it had been so drastically cut and reedited that it had little to do with my version. I was never consulted, and I never found out who was responsible for cutting it. Cutting out the material about the other characters caused the picture to look like a continual pantomime, with Gleason following himself in a series of sketches. He was brokenhearted about it. We thought we had a minor classic—but not as it stands."

Showing Jacques Marin how to help the drunken Gigot from the bar

WHAT A WAY TO GO

CREDITS:

A J. Lee Thompson Production, released by 20th Century-Fox 1964. Produced by Arthur P. Jacobs. Directed by J. Lee Thompson. Screenplay by Betty Comden and Adolph Green, based on a story by Gwen Davis. Photographed in CinemaScope and De Luxe Color by Leom Shamroy. Art direction by Jack Martin Smith and Ted Haworth. Edited by Marjorie Fowler. Musical score by Nelson Riddle. Running time: 111 minutes.

CAST:

Louisa: Shirley MacLaine; *Larry Flint:* Paul Newman; *Rod Anderson:* Robert Mitchum; *Leonard Crawley:* Dean Martin; *Jerry Benson:* Gene Kelly; *Dr. Stephenson:* Bob Cummings; *Edgar Hopper:* Dick Van Dyke; *Painter:* Reginald Gardiner; *Mrs. Foster:* Margaret Dumont; *Trentino:* Lou Nova; *Baroness:* Fifi D'Orsay; *Rene:* Maurice Marsac; *Agent:* Wally Vernon; *Polly:* Jane Wald; *Hollywood lawyer:* Lenny Kent.

What a Way to Go is a textbook example of all that was wrong with Hollywood in the mid-1960s. Supposedly a satire on the evils of affluence and abundance, the film was sunk by its own excesses, one of them being the assumption that humor can be drawn from death, if a man dies in a funny situation. Some of the studios at this time were misled by the public's apparent appetite for movies, thinking that the great slump of the fifties was over. Such was not quite the case. The public, saturated with mediocre entertainment on television, were eager for films on the particular rather than the general level. 20th Cen-

214

tury-Fox make the mistake of imagining that *The Sound of Music* heralded the revival of the movie musical, and in a strange moment of antiquated reasoning that same studio assumed that the surest way to make a comedy hilarious would be to spend five million dollars on it. *What a Way to Go* proved anything but.

The film is a group of stories with a single theme —a woman with the Midas touch, who makes a millionaire of every man she marries, but finds that great wealth leads each one to his death. Louisa Benson (Shirley MacLaine) tries to hand over her vast fortune to the Internal Revenue Service, to be free of the curse of money, but the government considers her mad and declines the offer. The distraught woman tells her sad tale to an incredulous psychiatrist, Dr. Stephenson (Robert Cummings).

The daughter of a money-hungry mother, Louisa spurns a rich suitor, Leonard Crawley (Dean Martin) and marries instead a humble storekeeper, Edgar Hopper (Dick Van Dyke). Their simple lifestyle is ridiculed by Crawley, and Hopper is taunted into making something of himself. He becomes a successful merchant and works and works until he drops dead—leaving a fortune. Louisa goes to Paris to forget but meets and marries a struggling American painter, Larry Flint (Paul Newman), who has invented a machine to paint pictures, its arms being driven by sound-waves. Louisa has the idea of feeding classical music into the machine, which results in master-pieces in profusion. This brings wealth—and death to Larry, when he gets caught up in the arms of the machine, leaving an even richer widow.

Louisa next marries a wealthy industrialist, Rod Anderson (Robert Mitchum), thinking that an already rich man will have nothing to fear from her. They both decide to get away from it all by living a simple life running a little farm in the country, but Rod's neglect of his empire ironically causes it to expand and the poor man is killed when, out of sheer ignorance, he tries to milk a bull.

Newly widowed, Louisa happens to visit a dingy nightclub as the entertainer is doing his act. This is Jerry Benson (Gene Kelly), known to friends as Pinky because of his fixation on the color pink, who does a clown act and does it so badly the customers ignore him. But he is a happy, carefree soul with no ambition—until he falls in love with Louisa and marries her. One evening, with not enough time to get into his costume and his grotesque makeup, Pinky goes on the floor and does his act as a straight ballad, to the approval

With Shirley MacLaine

With Shirley MacLaine

215

of the audience. His career blossoms and he goes from success to success until he becomes a Hollywood star, the kind who does lavish song-and-dance numbers in splendid settings. He does one of them with his wife, a nautical musical with squads of singers and dancers cavorting over the vast deck of a battleship. Pinky is a smash with the public and everything in his life is pink—his home, his wife's clothes and his car—even the coffin he needs after his adoring fans have trampled him to

With Shirley MacLaine

With Shirley MacLaine

217

death. As Louisa finishes telling her story to Dr. Stephenson he receives a call from the Internal Revenue Service advising him her story is genuine and that they will accept her wealth—news which causes him to faint. The janitor enters the scene, and turns out to be Leonard Crawley, now devoid of funds due to business failures. He and Louisa marry, and live in happy poverty.

The four husband-stories are partly told in the style of various past movie periods—silent, European, Hollywood plush, etc.—but in ribbing old failings the producers of this picture are blind to their own. Allocating, as here, half a million dollars for costumes impresses few other than those who work on the production, and the device of using stars in cameo roles had lost its novelty long before this film was conceived. A movie skit within this movie is labeled a "Lush Budget Production," but the joke hardly comes across under the egregious circumstances.

The best-realized material in *What a Way to Go* is Gene Kelly's knowing lampoon of his own kind of image. The character and the devices are suggestive of *Singin' in the Rain,* which is not surprising, seeing that the scenarists are Comden and Green. The music for the "Musical Extravaganza" was written by Jule Styne, a veteran composer for the American musical, and Kelly devised the choreography. This splendidly dreadful number was an affectionate dig at Busby Berkeley but it is also reminiscent of what another dancer did in *Follow the Fleet.*

With Françoise Dorlèac

THE YOUNG GIRLS OF ROCHEFORT

CREDITS:

A Co-Production of Parc Films, Madeleine Films and Seven Arts, released in the United States by Warner Bros. 1968. Produced by Mag Bodard. Direction, screenplay and lyrics by Jacques Demy. Music composed and conducted by Michel Legrand. Choreography by Norman Maen. Photographed in Franscope and Technicolor by Ghislain Cloquet. Art direction by Bernard Evein. Edited by Jean Hamon. Running time, 126 minutes.

CAST:

Delphine Garnier: Catherine Deneuve; *Solange Garnier:* Françoise Dorléac; *Étienne:* George Chakiris; *Bill:* Grover Dale; *Andy Miller:* Gene Kelly; *Yvonne:* Danielle Darrieux; *Maxence:* Jacques

Perrin; *Simon Dame:* Michel Piccoli; *Judith:* Pamela Hart; *Esther:* Leslie North; *Guillaume Lancien:* Jacques Riberolles; *Dutrouz:* Henri Crémieux; *Boubou:* Patrick Jeantet; *Josette:* Geneviève Thénier.

Although it is obviously Gallic in tone and character, *The Young Girls of Rochefort* is a sincere homage to the Hollywood musical, even to the extent of having Gene Kelly as one of its central figures. Unfortunately the presence of Kelly tends to accentuate the fact that the film fails to emulate the genre it tries to respect. It is pleasing to look at, but it is soft and formless. Writer-director Jacques Demy, a film maker who apparently looks at the world through a rose-colored range-finder, spread his thin story over two hours of screen time and made the mistake of hiring a choreographer, Norman Maen, with very little film experience. The dancing has vitality but it fails to take advantage of the space available in Rochefort, particularly in the huge Colbert Square. The dancers cluster in front of the camera, as they would on a stage, rather than besport themselves through the town. The dancing done in the film by Kelly was devised and staged by himself.

Another deficiency in *The Young Girls of Rochefort* is the music of Michel Legrand, a lengthy score containing more than a dozen songs and five pieces for dancing. Legrand had provided a tuneful score for Demy's charming *The Umbrellas of Cherbourg,* but *Rochefort* failed to fire the prolific composer-arranger. The music, as always with Legrand, has considerable style but in this instance a dulling sameness. The film badly needed a few hit songs, if only to promote it, but there were none. The story called for a flashy, modern piano concerto and Legrand, a gifted pianist, provided a piece that works well within the confines of the picture but not distinctive enough to have a life of its own. Sadly, it is this lack of impressive music that will cause the film to fade into limbo.

As he had in Cherbourg, Demy changed the

With Catherine Deneuve

With Catherine Deneuve

220

With Françoise Dorlèac

face of the town for the better. Once he decided on Rochefort as his location, having considered many other towns, Demy persuaded the town council to let him paint many of the houses and stores in pastel colors. Rochefort, a town of thirty thousand population on the southwest coast of France, is noted mainly as a fishing port and a market for wine and oysters and not as a particular point of interest for tourists. But after Demy's gilding, the town took on a new attractiveness.

The young girls of the title are the Garnier twins, Solange (Françoise Dorléac) and Delphine (Catherine Deneuve). Both are highly romantic in their attitudes toward life and both are musical —Solange teaches various musical instruments and Delphine teaches dancing. Their unmarried mother, Yvonne (Danielle Darrieux) runs a little cafe and dreams of her long-lost lover, Simon Dame (Michel Piccoli), who, unknown to her, operates a music shop in Rochefort. A theatrical company, headed by Étienne (George Chakiris) and Bill (Grover Dale) arrive in the town and set up a fair in Colbert Square. When two of their girl dancers quit, the boys look around for replacements and soon discover Solange and Delphine.

The twins immediately become the stars of the

221

show, although they decline the friendship of their employers and continue to dream about their ideal men. Such men soon turn up—a handsome young sailor named Maxence (Jacques Perrin), an artist when not in national service and who has painted a portrait of his dream girl, who, by a great coincidence resembles Delphine. The other man is an American concert pianist, Andy Miller (Gene Kelly), who has discovered the score of a piano concerto, which, by another coincidence, happens to be the lost property of composer Solange. The lives of all these people intertwine for a few days, producing a few complications and much singing and dancing. Eventually the entertainers leave the town and the two girls find the romance they wished for in the arms of the sailor and the pianist. Their mother also reunites with Monsieur Dame. Demy pads the flimsy plotline with a few characterizations of townspeople, including a rather unnecessary one of a sadistic killer who carves up women who reject him, but the charm and the wit are strained in this long session in a far-from-fascinating little town.

For Gene Kelly *The Young Girls of Rochefort* is a keenly felt disappointment, particularly so in that Demy clearly meant the enterprise as a tribute to the kind of film Kelly had once made. Demy asked Kelly to be in the film, and in agreeing to take the part Demy was therefore able to raise American financing. Kelly's role in this large soufflé is that of a brash but likable American, an older version of the one in Paris sixteen years previously, and he carried it off with ease. Says Kelly: "It was a good idea, a nice, lyrical concept but it missed. I think Demy made a major mistake in casting Catherine Deneuve and Françoise Dorléac. The parts needed girls of exceptional dancing and singing ability but neither Catherine or Françoise could sing and they had no dancing experience. Almost everyone in the picture had to be dubbed—Daniele Darrieux was about the only one of the leads whose singing voice could be used —and this puts a great strain on a musical. And they all made the mistake of assuming that it's easy to learn to dance for a film, because it looks so easy. It isn't."

With Françoise Dorlèac

With Françoise Dorlèac

Directions for Walter Matthau and Inger Stevens

A GUIDE FOR THE MARRIED MAN

CREDITS:

A 20th Century-Fox Production 1967. Produced by Frank McCarthy. Directed by Gene Kelly. Screenplay by Frank Tarloff, based on his book. Photographed in Panavision and De Luxe Color by Joe MacDonald. Art direction by Jack Martin Smith and William Glasgow. Edited by Dorothy Spencer. Musical score by Johnny Williams. Running time: 89 minutes.

CAST:

Paul Manning: Walter Matthau; *Ed Stander:* Robert Morse; *Ruth Manning:* Inger Stevens; *Irma Johnson:* Sue Ane Langdon; *Harriet Stander:* Claire Kelly; *Miss Stardust:* Linda Harrison; *Jocelyn Montgomery:* Elaine Devry.

224

GUEST STARS: Lucille Ball, Jack Benny, Polly Bergen, Joey Bishop, Ben Blue, Sid Caesar, Art Carney, Wally Cox, Marty Ingels, Ann Morgan Guilbert, Jeffrey Hunter, Sam Jaffe, Jayne Mansfield, Hal March, Louis Nye, Carl Reiner, Phil Silvers and Terry-Thomas.

Sex is not easy to spoof, particularly those areas of it dealing with infidelity, but Gene Kelly came close to perfection with *A Guide for the Married Man*, a film that might have sunk in a mire of tastelessness in less cunning hands. The charm of the film is that it leers without being lewd, it ogles pretty girls in genuine appreciation and while it seemingly sets out as a statement of man's triumph over woman it ends up as anything but. The joke of Kelly's *Guide* is on men, not women.

A Guide for the Married Man is a Hollywood factory product on an expert level. It shines with professional skills, beginning with animated credit titles which touch on the history of the battle of the sexes. Several panels reveal famous quotations, the most apposite being Oscar Wilde's wicked observation: "The one charm of marriage is that it makes a life of deception absolutely necessary for both parties." The color photography of the late Joe MacDonald moves through dozens of attractive locations in Beverly Hills and Los Angeles, catching glimpses of a great variety of young ladies, and the film is paced by Kelly at a brisk clip. The directorial style is suggestive of his musicals, and *Guide* emerges rather like *On the Town* minus the singing and the dancing. The visual aspect of the film is complicated but thanks to the editing of Dorothy Spencer it is also smooth, and backed all the way by the richly comedic score of Johnny Williams.

The film is almost without plot. It deals mainly with the advice of one man to another, and his points are illustrated, both positively and negatively, by a stream of enacted situations featuring famous Hollywood faces. A genial, faithful and happily married man, Paul Manning (Walter Matthau) wonders what it would be like to have an affair with another woman, despite the fact that his wife Ruth (Inger Stevens) is pretty, devoted and perpetually pleasant. No sooner does he start to wonder than his libidinous friend and neighbor, Ed Stander (Robert Morse) begins to proffer advice. Ed considers himself a master of extramarital liaisons, an expert in the art of manipulating women, and he theorizes that a man makes a better husband if he maintains a healthy interest in other women, provided his wife doesn't know about it.

Goaded and encouraged by Ed, Paul decides to take his first fling at adultery. He settles for a handsome, wealthy and willing divorcee named Jocelyn Montgomery (Elaine Devry) and proceeds to rendezvous with her in a remote motel. Once alone with the statuesque Jocelyn, who wastes no time in stripping down to her underwear, Paul loses his nerve and immediately confesses he is a married man. "Congratulations" says the cool lady, intent on the tryst. Paul's predicament is interrupted by a commotion in another part of the hotel. Looking out of a window he sees a room being broken into by Mrs. Ed Stander and her witnesses. Inside the room Ed and his date peer from the bedcovers in horrified embarrassment.

A lesson in seductive walking for Sue Ann Langdon

With photographer Joe MacDonald

225

Instructions for a Go-Go dancer

With Jack Benny

Seeing his tutor so ignominiously defeated Paul, frantically nervous, dashes for his rented car, dragging the half-clad Jocelyn behind him and drives away. He dumps Jocelyn at the car rental lot, climbs into his own convertible and speeds home. As Paul rushes into the arms of his wife, a celestial chorus sings "There's No Place Like Home."

The performance of Walter Matthau is the solid platform on which the humor of the film rests. As a plain, ordinary, decent Everyman Matthau is fully understandable in his anguish. His Paul is a home-loving man only mildly discontented with his lot, and pushed into philandering only after much persuasion. His amiable playing is a good foil for perky Robert Morse as the impish astray-leader, and the late Inger Stevens is so lovely, so kind and so accommodating as the wife that the audience has cause to wonder why the husband would stray. A partial answer to that puzzle is given in one of the picture's many one-line gags. Marty Ingels is seen eating a steak; he holds up a piece and says, "This is the best steak money can buy. But every now and then I feel like fish."

Gene Kelly's direction of *A Guide for the Married Man* is commendable for several reasons, not the least being his decision to pack the proceedings into a brief hour-and-a-half of running time. Within that period a large number of guest stars pop up to illuminate the points given by the *Guide*. Many of them are so brief they are hardly worth the effort of employing a famous name but a few of the stars appear to advantage in vignettes that make good use of their talents. Perhaps the best is Art Carney, as a lusty construction worker who picks on the cooking of wife Lucille Ball in order to provoke her into saying, "If you don't like the food here, go somewhere else." He goes elsewhere, has an enjoyable evening with a girl-friend, and comes home the next day to apologize for his ingratitude.

Jack Benny appears in his familiar guise as a tightwad, pleading financial disaster and suggesting to his mistress that they sell off various pieces of jewelry and clothing to bring in funds. The mistress replies that perhaps they shouldn't see each other for a while, and Jack painfully agrees —while cocking an eye out the window to a new girlfriend sitting in his car. Terry-Thomas illustrates the mistake of entertaining girlfriend Jayne Mansfield in his own home; he is reduced to a nervous wreck by not being able to find her

Directions for Walter Matthau and Inger Stevens

brassiere. Joey Bishop demonstrates how to behave when discovered by the wife in bed with another woman—pretend, with total conviction, that there is no other woman present.

The film's most lavish sketch has Carl Reiner as a hammy Hollywood matinee idol, being so cautious in his amorous plotting that he and a starlet set out for a rendezvous in a snowbound Swiss chalet by going opposite ways around the world to get there—only to have his wife walk in on them, complete with cameramen. *A Guide for the Married Man* is, of course, no guide at all, and therein lies its fun.

The director on location, at a tea room owned by a namesake

HELLO DOLLY

CREDITS:

A Chenault Production, released by 20th Century-Fox 1969. Produced and written for the screen by Ernest Lehman. Directed by Gene Kelly, Associate Producer: Roger Edens. Dances and musical numbers staged by Michael Kidd. Based on the musical play by Michael Stewart and *The Matchmaker* by Thornton Wilder. Music and lyrics by Jerry Herman. Music direction by Lennie Hayton and Lionel Newman. Photographed in TODD-AO and De Luxe Color by Harry Stradling. Art direction by Jack Martin Smith and Herman Blumenthal. Edited by William Reynolds. Running time: 149 minutes.

CAST:

Dolly Levi: Barbra Streisand; *Horace Vander-gelder:* Walter Matthau; *Cornelius Hackl:* Michael Crawford; *Orchestra Leader:* Louis Armstrong; *Irene Molloy:* Marianne McAndrew; *Minnie Fay:* E. J. Peaker; *Barnaby Tucker:* Danny Lockin; *Ermenarde:* Joyce Ames; *Ambrose Kemper:* Tommy Tune; *Gussie Granger:* Judy Knaiz; *Rudolph Reisenweber:* David Hurst; *Fritz:* Fritz Feld; *Vandergelder's Barber:* Richard Collier; *Policeman in Park:* J. Pat O'Malley.

Late in 1965, seduced by the flow of millions of dollars profit on *The Sound of Music,* 20th Century-Fox proceeded to set up plans for three expensive musicals. It was the greatest mistake so far made in the history of the film industry. Fox spent twenty million dollars on *Star,* with Julie Andrews playing Gertrude Lawrence, and nearly eighteen million on *Dr. Doolittle,* starring Rex

Harrison. Both were staggering flops and it is doubtful if they will ever realize even half their original costs. Fox compounded this folly by buying the screen rights to *Hello Dolly* for two million dollars and signing a contract with owner David Merrick to the effect that the completed film could not be shown until the original Broadway production closed, or June 20, 1971, whichever came first. The show had already run three years at the time of this agreement and no one at Fox imagined it would run on and on. The film was finished by late summer, 1968, and then sat on the shelf for more than a year with the studio paying interest on the film's financing at the rate of $100,000 per month. Fox threatened to release the film and Merrick countered with a legal suit. Merrick, with money pouring in from every direction, wanted to keep Broadway's *Dolly* running until it broke the record set by *My Fair Lady*. In desperation Fox offered to come to terms with him and in a settlement that allowed them to issue the film in December of 1969 the studio paid David Merrick a further one million dollars.

The final cost of the film is known only to the accountants and management of 20th Century-Fox but it is estimated to be between twenty and twenty-five million dollars. The choice of actress to play the lead was a point of considerable interest after Fox made known its purchase of the property. Choosing Barbra Streisand caused quite a commotion, mostly because at twenty-six she was obviously a different image from the requirements of the role as written—and played on stage by such celebrated middle-aged veterans as Mary Martin, Ginger Rogers and Betty Grable. Much of the point of the story lies in Dolly Gallagher Levi being a warmhearted "older" woman, and in the minds of the public the personification of that role was Carol Channing, who had played it for the better part of four years. However, Miss Channing's charm had never been successfully captured on film, the rather bizarre personality and the raspy voice that work so effectively on stage tends to be grotesque in the intimacy of the camera. Ironically, Barbra Streisand had shown little interest in the vehicle. After being signed for the film she told reporters she considered the musical play, "A piece of fluff. But when everybody was against me as Dolly I took up the challenge."

The story of Dolly Levi, invented by Thorton Wilder for his play *The Matchmaker*, was filmed under that title by Paramount in 1958 with Shirley Booth beautifully cast as the turn-of-the-century

On location in the Hudson Valley, New York. Kelly at left with megaphone

With Barbra Streisand

229

With Walter Matthau

With Walter Matthau and
Barbra Streisand

230

widow who can't resist playing Cupid. Her match-making becomes almost a profession, but in ostensibly trying to find a mate for a wealthy merchant named Horace Vandergelder she moves to nab him for her own. This was also the core of Michael Stewart's musical version, with lyrics and music by Jerry Herman, and in making this into a film, writer-producer Ernest Lehman made little alteration other than making Dolly a younger woman and physically opening up the play to allow for enormous photographic treatment. For the part of Vandergelder Fox selected the popular Walter Matthau, but this move backfired to a minor degree by the inability of Matthau and Streisand to work together amicably. Early in the production they began to quarrel, he calling her Miss Ptomaine and she calling him Old Sewer-Mouth, with director Kelly having to pacify both.

Gene Kelly: "It wasn't until we were well into the picture that I realized Barbra was uncom-fortable. I asked her why and she admitted she was scared of the part, feeling, like most everybody else, that she was too young for Dolly. She said she thought Elizabeth Taylor would have been a better choice. I had to reassure her and explain that she had to find ways to make up for this change in concept, to look for other things in the part, and she did. But she was very insecure. I had some trepidation about working with her because she had a reputation for being difficult but I didn't find her so. I asked William Wyler and Vincente Minnelli if they had had any problems with her and they said they hadn't. I'd been told she had had some people fired but I couldn't find any proof of that either. She certainly is direct in her manner and her opinions but I prefer that."

Unfortunately, by the time the film was released the public's fascination with the subject of Dolly Levi and the popularity of the songs had diminished. *Hello Dolly* made no where near the

Rehearsing Barbra Streisand

impact the producers hoped for and it has yet to show signs of recouping its hefty costs. It may do this, in time. However, there is much to recommend the picture, certainly from a visual standpoint. Fox spent a further two million dollars turning the main street of its Beverly Hills studio into a New York thoroughfare in the 1890s, and for the mammoth street parade sequence in this setting they hired four thousand extras. According to Kelly it was like having a standing army at his disposal, at a cost of $200,000 per day, a frightening responsibility. The company was on location at Garrison, New York, a little town on the banks of the Hudson River and another half million dollars was spent beautifying the town.

It is a genial, handsome, old-fashioned musical dogged by bad luck in its timing and in the decision to spend so much money making it. Its director admits: "It's not the kind of film I would make as a first choice but what else is there? To make an original musical today you first have to find someone to put up a million dollars just to develop the idea, and that's too much of a risk. What happens now is that studios buy stage shows after they are already dated and then spend a lot of money turning them into dated movies. The musical is the victim of changing times. To make good musicals you need a team of performers, musicians, costume and set designers, choreographers, writers and arrangers, etc., etc. In short, what we used to have at MGM. Well, it's no longer possible. The economics of the business have killed all that. It's all too easy to ridicule Fox for spending all that money making *Dolly* but they took a brave stand—they had spent so much getting hold of the property that they wanted to turn it into a whale of a good show. It takes guts to make that kind of a decision, and as the director I was excited by the challenge of blowing it up into a big and exciting picture. I'm not sorry I did it."

With James Stewart

THE CHEYENNE SOCIAL CLUB

CREDITS:

A National General Production 1970. Produced and directed by Gene Kelly. Screenplay by James Lee Barrett. Photographed in Panavision and Technicolor by William Clother. Art direction by Gene Allen. Edited by Adrienne Fazan. Musical score by Walter Scharf. Running time: 103 minutes.

CAST:

John O'Hanlan: James Stewart; *Harley Sullivan:* Henry Fonda; *Jenny:* Shirley Jones; *Opal Ann:* Sue Ane Langdon; *Willouby:* Dabbs Greer; *Pauline:* Elaine Devry; *Barkeep:* Robert Middleton; *Marshall Anderson:* Arch Johnson; *Carrie Virginia:* Jackie Russell; *Annie Jo:* Jackie Joseph; *Sara Jean:* Sharon De Bord; *Nathan Potter:* Rich-ard Collier; *Charlie Bannister:* Charles Tyner; *Alice:* Jean Willes; *Corey Bannister:* Robert J. Wilke; *Pete Dodge:* Carl Reindel; *Dr. Foy:* J. Pat O'Malley; *Dr. Carter:* Jason Wingreen; *Clay Carrol:* John Dehner.

James Stewart brought the script of *The Cheyenne Social Club* to Gene Kelly and asked him if he would be interested in making the picture. Kelly took a liking to the script and said he would do it, provided Henry Fonda could be persuaded to co-star with Stewart. This condition was easily met, and a company was set up with Kelly as producer-director and scriptwriter James Lee Barrett as the executive producer. Barrett had written several of Stewart's previous films and he had acquired a reputation as a man with a particular talent for Western dialogue and characterizations.

With Henry Fonda and James Stewart

James Stewart and Henry Fonda

This is apparent from the very outset in *The Cheyenne Social Club*, as two grizzled old cowpokes, Harley Sullivan (Fonda) and John O'Hanlan (Stewart) slowly make their way across a vast landscape. The voice of Harley is heard droning on and on and on . . . about his family and his dogs and his doings. John, a long-suffering listener, finally gets a chance to speak. "You know where we are now, Harley?" "Not exactly." "We're in the Wyoming territory and you've been talkin' all the way from Texas." Harley looks wounded. "Just been keepin' you company." Replies John, "I appreciate it, Harley, but if you say another word the rest of the day I'm gonna kill you."

The two old cowboys are making their way to Cheyenne because John has received an inheritance from a deceased brother, although he doesn't exactly know what it is. It turns out to be a social club, but even with that news he is unaware of the true nature of his fortune—a plush bordello, staffed with half a dozen lovely girls, and the center of life in the town. The madam is Jenny (Shirley Jones), and she and the girls make their new boss welcome, with Harley accepted as a part-

Henry Fonda, James Stewart, Sue Ann Langdon, Elaine Devry, Jackie Russell, Jackie Joseph, Sharon De Bord and Shirley Jones

ner, although he doesn't do anything except enjoy the hospitality of the house. The amiable Harley takes life as it comes, but John is a straitlaced old bachelor and the idea of running the place bothers him. One morning at breakfast John tells the girls he aims to change the house into a respectable saloon and that they will have to leave. The girls

With Shirley Jones and James Stewart

With James Stewart

are dismayed, but not nearly as dismayed as the local citizens, whose respect for him suddenly turns to scorn.

John is forced to change his mind about selling his social club when he realizes what will happen to Jenny and the girls. He himself is set upon in a barroom and after beating his opponents he is thrown in the local jail. Meanwhile Jenny is beaten by an outlaw, Corey Bannister (Robert J. Wilke) and to avenge her John seeks out Bannister and guns him down. This regains the respect of the citizenry, but it also brings an attack on his establishment by the entire Bannister clan of six brothers and sundry hirelings. Harley, away for a while, arrives back in time to help John and the girls win their battle, but having banished the Bannisters they then learn that more related bandits will descend upon them. Not willing to engage in any more warfare John signs over the social club to Jenny, and he and Harley take their leave, drifting back into the landscape as a kind of Western "Odd Couple," with John presumably doomed to spend his remaining years impatiently listening to the nonstop drawl of Harley.

The Cheyenne Social Club is a good-looking picture, not just because of its girls but through the expertise of veteran cinematographer William Clother, a man with a feeling for the western scene. The budget was set at three million dollars and production designer Gene Allen spent a quarter million of it building a vintage town on the J. W. Eaves Ranch, near Santa Fe, New Mexico. The film has a plausible, genial feel to it, but it did not receive quite the response the producers had hoped. Says Kelly: "Many people considered our bordello too nice and the girls too attractive, thinking that nothing this good could have existed in the real West. Actually, there were houses like this. The wealthy cattlemen and railroad men did indeed set up plush social clubs, calling them that, and they hired only pretty, classy girls. We also ran into another problem with the picture: many people didn't take to the idea of Jimmy Stewart in this setting, it was counter-image. We had one bedroom scene in which Jimmy is approached by a girl wearing a see-through negligee. It seemed funny at the time but looking at it later we both felt it should come out. But the owners, National General, insisted it stay, and I think that was a mistake."

With James Stewart and Henry Fonda

FORTY CARATS

CREDITS:

A Columbia Picture 1973. Produced by M. J. Frankovich. Directed by Milton Katselas. Written by Leonard Gershe, based on a play by Pierre Barillet and Jean-Pierre Gredy, adapted by Jay Allen. Photographed in Metrocolor by Charles B. Lang. Production designer, Robert Clatworthy. Edited by David Blewitt. Musical score by Michael Legrand. Running time: 108 minutes.

CAST:

Ann Stanley: Liv Ullmann; *Peter Latham:* Edward Albert; *Billy Boylan:* Gene Kelly; *Maud Ericson:* Binnie Barnes; *Trina Stanley:* Deborah Raffin; *J. D. Rogers:* Billy Green Bush; *Mrs. Margolin:* Nancy Walker; *Mr. Latham:* Don Porter; *Mrs. Latham:* Rosemary Murphy; *Mrs. Adams:* Natalie Schaefer; *Arthur Forbes:* Sam Chew, Jr.; *Gabriella:* Claudia Jennings; *Polly:* Brooks Palance.

Difficult, furtive and frustrating though the film business may be, good roles sometimes come to actors in an easy and simple way. Producer Mike Frankovich wanted Gene Kelly for the part of Billy Boylan in *Forty Carats,* but hesitated to offer what was essentially a supporting role to an actor-director of star status. Kelly accepted the role even without seeing the script. "I couldn't see myself declining the opportunity to work with Liv Ullmann, an enchanting actress. Mike said I'd probably want to see the script before I *really* said yes, and I told him to forget it. I think he thought I was putting him on but I wasn't. I wanted to work in a film with that wonderful actress and that was

239

With Liv Ullman

With Natalie Schafer

enough." The role of Billy Boylan is not a large one but, as Kelly says: "That's not the point. It's good material and it's time we in Hollywood got away from this pretentious business of labeling the appearance of a star in a small part as a *cameo,* as if excusing it. Casting people to type has always been the curse of this business and so has the star syndrome—a lot of talented actors have had their development curtailed by becoming stars. The British and European actors are luckier in that respect, they are not nearly as hidebound or as locked-in as their American brothers."

Liv Ullmann had long been lauded for her work in Swedish films with the prestigious Ingmar Bergman, but it wasn't until her performance in the epic *The Emigrants* that Hollywood began to consider her as an actress of possible wide appeal. Ross Hunter hired her for his lavish but limp musical version of *Lost Horizon,* and after seeing some of the footage of that picture Frankovich decided that Miss Ullmann was the actress for *Forty Carats,* thereby disappointing a number of famed and aging Hollywood actresses. At the age of thirty-seven she was actually too young to play the role, that of a middle-aged woman falling in love with a man young enough to be her son. But, as Kelly explains, "Once Mike had seen Liv, there were suddenly no contenders," and he instructed scenarist Leonard Gershe to alter the part accordingly.

Forty Carats, a French play, was first seen in Paris in late 1967. Among those who saw and liked it was David Merrick, and he purchased the American rights, commissioning Jay Allen to adapt the play into English. It was a hit of the 1968–9 Broadway season and subsequent touring companies. Its romantic plot premise is one common in life, but seldom before touched upon in films. Ann Stanley (Ullmann) is a successful Manhattan real estate agent who meets a personable young American, Peter Latham (Edward Albert), during a vacation in Greece. At first hesitant about his attraction to her, she gradually succumbs to his charm and spends a night with him on a beach. In the morning, before he awakes, she steals away. Some months later, by pure coincidence, Peter turns up at Ann's apartment as a date for her daughter Trina (Deborah Raffin). She discovers that Peter is a brilliant young business executive from a good social background, something which greatly impresses her modish mother Maud (Binnie Barnes), who supports the boy in his campaign to win Ann. Ann tries to deny her own affection for Peter

240

With Binnie Barnes

With Binnie Barnes and Liv Ullman

but finds nothing but arguments in favor of the affair—from her mother, her daughter, her sardonic business partner (Nancy Walker), and even from her ex-husband Billy Boylan (Kelly). Eventually Ann surrenders to these arguments, and to her love for Peter, and agrees to marry him.

The title of the play derives from a conversation between Ann and Billy. He is, despite their divorce, still greatly fond of her and concerned about her happiness. She bemoans the age difference between Peter and herself, and laments the fact that she is forty years old. Billy replies, "Don't think of it like that. Think like a diamond. Not years—carats. You're a multi-carated blue-white."

Although Gene Kelly had vowed not to take any more dancing roles in films he did agree to a short sequence in *Forty Carats,* in which Boylan and Maud do a fast-tempo dance to a rock beat in a discotheque. The veteran Binnie Barnes had never before danced in a film, but both she and Kelly appeared in fine form in this amusing moment. The age-defying little dance was in keeping with the character of Billy Boylan, a lighthearted, cheerful but shallow actor pretending to be a decade younger than his years. Boylan is the kind of actor who operates on personality and never quite reaches the level of success that would enable

him to relax his quest for work. In essaying such a character, Kelly clearly drew on many years of close observation.

Forty Carats did not win much favor with the critics. The major magazines dismissed it slick as entertainment, only glibly touching on the problems of age-gap marriages. However, public response was sufficiently strong to assure the producers of profit. The critical reaction to the performance of Liv Ullmann was one of disappointment. In reviewing the picture for the Toronto *Star* Clyde Gilmour sounded a generally felt impression:

Mainly, I think, this is because the talented and delectable Miss Ullmann just doesn't seem to have a talent for comedy. She looks beautiful, and it's not hard to imagine a man of twenty-two falling madly in love with her, but she often seems a bit harried and ill-at-ease in the midst of supposedly hilarious episodes.

Gilmour also commented: "To the film's credit, be it noted that Gene Kelly's work as the irrepressible ex-husband is warm and winning." Kelly won approval from most critics and *Variety* went so far as to claim this one of his finest characterizations:

He projects superbly the intricacies of a showbiz character, an aging gypsy so to speak, whose head and heart are together though his career is erratic. It's made to order for his mature abilities in both comedy and drama . . .

Hollywood had probably assumed that because of his success as a producer and director Kelly was no longer interested in acting. His success in *Forty Carats* dispelled that impression and also guaranteed him further roles. During the filming Kelly admitted that it was something of a luxury to be in front of the cameras again, rather than behind them: "When you're a director, you're working every minute, shouldering all that responsibility. On top of that, by the time you prepare a film, shoot it and edit it, that's more than a year out of your life. But as an actor, you rehearse, do your scenes, collect your money and go home. Lovely!" Kelly also admitted that he had let his acting career slide in favor of his family life. "I've turned down some tempting roles the last couple of years because the pictures were being done away off some place. I'm a family man and my kids are in school. I'm not going to uproot them, nor am I going to miss the joy of being with them."

As to what he feels he has yet to accomplish Gene Kelly replies, "A lot. One thing I would like to do is sort of review my career by putting together a clip of everything I've done. Then sit back and appraise it—and from seeing where I've been perhaps I'll decide where I'm going."

With Liv Ullman